To my friends who have helped me along the way,
and to Teddie, my wife and steadfast partner.

RAY ELLIS

To all those who go down to the sea in ships,
in pursuit of our commerce or in defense of it,
for they are the keepers of an American heritage.

WALTER CRONKITE

NORTH BY NORTHEAST

RAY ELLIS/ WALTER CRONKITE

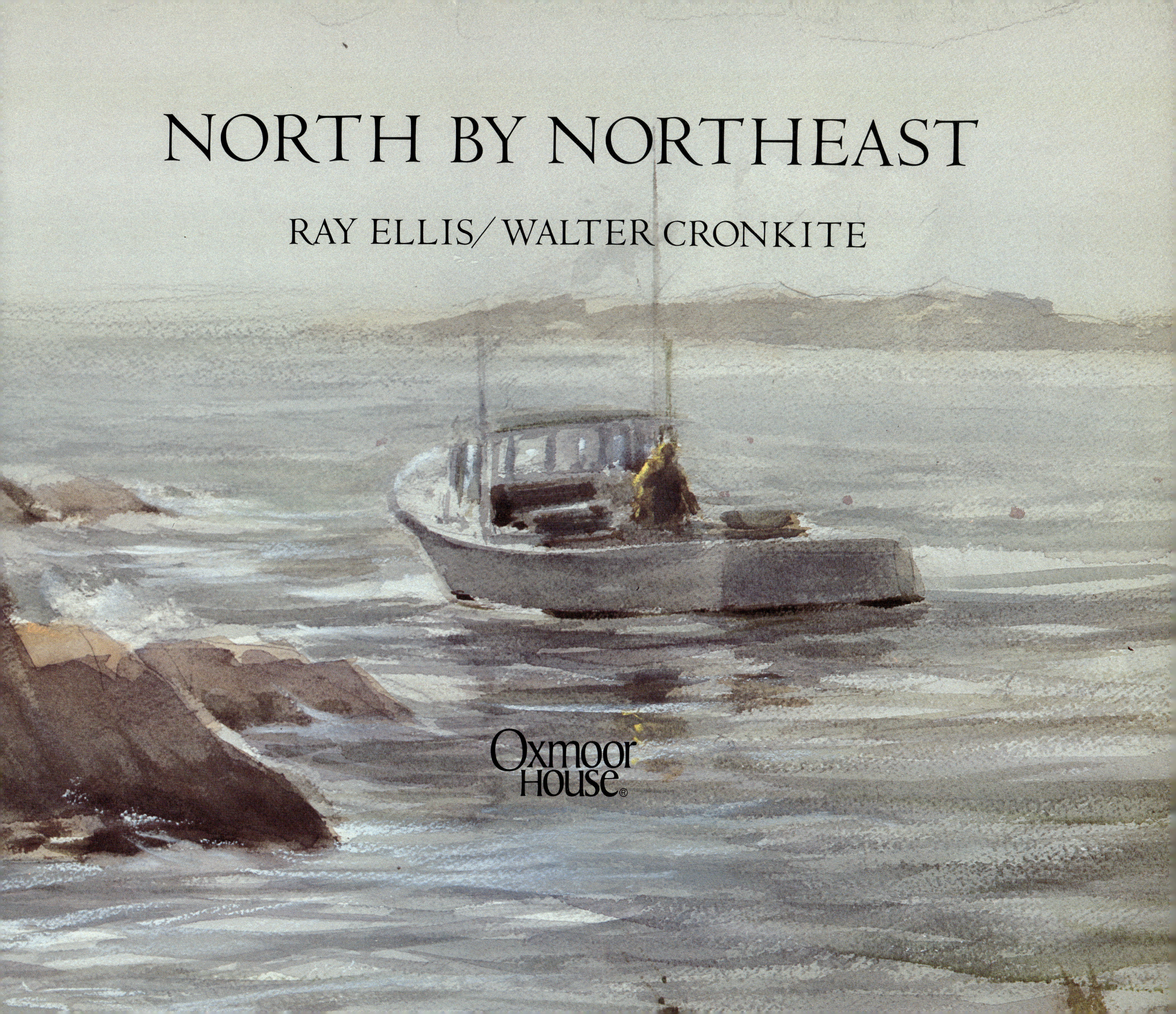

Oxmoor House®

Alone.

Book Division of Southern Progress Corporation
P.O. Box 2463, Birmingham, Alabama 35201

Library of Congress Catalog Number: 85-52361
ISBN: 0-8487-0641-2
Manufactured in the United States of America
First Edition

Executive Editor: Candace Conard Bromberg
Production Manager: Jerry Higdon
Art Director: Bob Nance

NORTH BY NORTHEAST

Editor: Cecilia C. Robinson
Editorial Assistant: Margaret Allen Northen
Production Assistant: Rick Litton

TITLE PAGE:
Working the Ledges.

What an incredible gift has been bestowed upon me to be able to return to the part of the East Coast where I grew up and on whose shores I spent most summers of my adult life.

Many of the paintings in this book are of places that I saw forty-five years ago when I was on duty from Race Point to Quoddy Head in the U.S. Coast Guard. Returning to this area in my Bertram "sketchboat" as I prepared for the work in this book filled me with nostalgia and many happy memories. It was the Maine coast—with its rugged beauty—which first inspired me to paint seriously, and I vowed to return to it as often as I could to try to recapture this splendor in paint.

The Northeast Coast has never been far from my mind or my heart. Next summer I will begin spending five months of every year in a studio in the woods on Martha's Vineyard.

RAY ELLIS

One would have to start as a very young man and grow to be a very, very old one to do justice by pen or brush to all the harbors, coves, and wonders afloat and ashore of the New England Coast from Cape May to the Canadian border. Since Ray and I did not start at the initial end of that chronological scale and at this pace won't likely reach the other, our efforts here cannot be considered in any way a comprehensive gazetteer.

Ray, however, has caught the infinite variety of this vast area, to our minds America's most interesting coast. And perhaps I have succeeded in doing something of the same by selecting my favorite scenes, harbors, and people and recounting some experiences in a couple of decades of sailing these waters.

A great number of sailing friends pointed out after our earlier work that there is no such compass point as "south by southeast." Similarly, there is no "north by northeast." It is not the publisher's intention to designate a sailing direction but rather to indicate, with at least a slightly nautical flavor, a region about which we have painted and written. I don't think one should use our books, as superb as they are, as aids for navigation.

Whatever geographical and historical accuracy I have achieved is due, in large part, to the considerable editorial assistance of James McGlincy and Roz Kramer.

WALTER CRONKITE

3. *Sutton Place in Winter.*

OVERLEAF: 4. *Brant Point Beach.*

All sails are set and they are pulling nicely—the big Genoa, the staysail, the main, and the little mizzen balancing it all.

It has been like this all night long, a spanking southwesterly of fifteen knots off the port quarter, enough to give us a good turn of speed but not enough to give the Atlantic waves any real punch in their eight-mile fetch from the New Jersey coast. They impart just a little corkscrew effect to keep the helmsman awake in this dogwatch hour right before dawn.

This has been one of the rare perfect passages along the Jersey coast, where any wind from the eastern hemisphere can make the Atlantic mighty unpleasant and render the few inlets dangerous of entry.

On this night I'm sure that fresh in my crew's memory is one of my command decisions a few months before on our fall southbound passage. I decided then to seek shelter from an approaching hurricane by running the inlet at Atlantic City.

It was an arguable decision, as my crew's lively discussion proved. But I believed the alternative worse, and it was I—oh, the loneliness of command—who had to issue the ultimate order, the order which we all had the right at that moment to consider one possibly of life or death.

5. Through the Inlet.

It usually would be safer to ride out a hurricane at sea, but lured by a highly erroneous weather forecast (for which the weather bureau actually broadcast an apology the next day—a first in my memory), we already were so close to shore when the storm struck that I believed clawing our way back out to deep water was likely to be the less successful or, to put it more succinctly, the more dangerous option.

Not exactly comforting was the knowledge that the shoals we fast were approaching had been littered over the centuries with the carcasses of ships whose masters had failed their final crises here. In the eighteenth century, wreckers bent on pillage lured captains onto the beach with lanterns. Believing the lights were other ships in deeper water, unwary captains followed them to their destruction. It was said that the wreckers' children even prayed at night:

"God bless mom and pop and all us poor miserable sinners and send a ship ashore before mornin'."

So there we were running down on the inlet, the sandy shoals ready to trap us if we missed the narrow channel between the granite breakwaters. The driving rain blinded us as we strained to find those fingers of rock in the wind-driven scud that at times was as thick as fog.

With forty-five to fifty knots of wind blowing directly down that opening and twenty- to thirty-foot waves threatening to send us uncontrollably tumbling down their forward walls, our only course was to tack down toward the channel. But with each tack we lost ground, sideways, toward those breakwaters.

Our situation was about as precarious as it could get when our reefed staysail let go, and a moment later the mizzen sheet parted. That left our engine to do the job.

For ten frightening, seemingly endless minutes, *Wyntje* fought to clear the breakwaters. Now it was just a hundred yards to the comparative safety on the other side of those jagged rocks, but each succeeding wave threatened to crash us down upon them.

And then suddenly, it was done. We skimmed the rocks with only feet to spare and gained the safety of the calmer waters inside the inlet.

Our experience was captured by an Atlantic City *Press* photographer, who pictured our plight as he was recording the storm's waves bursting on the famed boardwalk, and Ray turned it into a painting—the beauty of which almost made worthwhile the whole adventure.

Atlantic City is one of the few major inlets along the one-hundred-mile New Jersey coast, and the others, such as Great Egg Harbor, Barnegat, and Manasquan, can be as treacherous when the following sea is running strong.

6. *Yellow Umbrella.*

7. Cape May Victorian.

When you are seemingly alone out there being tossed about by the wild Atlantic, it is not well to dwell on the fact that only an hour's sail away, right through those inlets and protected by New Jersey's long barrier beach, stretches a huge body of water called Barnegat Bay, and on its marvellously calm waters hundreds of sailboats out of such delightful colonial localities as Waretown, Cedar Run, Forked River, and Toms River are even at that moment cavorting with unworried abandon.

It may be easier for those in the seaside resorts such as Spring Lake and Asbury Park and Bay Head to appreciate something of the ocean sailor's experience, for although they bask most summer days under their umbrellas on one of the East Coast's great beaches, they too on those stormy days know the Atlantic's uglier moods.

8. Suppertime.

One day more than a quarter of a century ago when we were summering at Allenhurst, I called in an expert for advice on our crumbling seawall. He was a fine old Norwegian who had helped build and maintain many beachfront installations including, if I remember right, Atlantic City's Steel Pier. He recommended rebuilding the wall, but he said he couldn't guarantee whether the new wall would last a week or a hundred years.

"Mr. Cronkite," he said, his pale blue eyes staring out to sea, "I've been at war with that old lady out there for fifty-three years, and I haven't won a battle yet."

Of those New Jersey resorts, the southernmost, down where the shore doubles back up Delaware Bay, is perhaps the most interesting. Cape May is a determinedly antique town that carries off its presumption with uncommon success.

9. *Beach at Bay Head.*

10. Day at the Beach.

Gasoline buggies with their noxious fumes can choke the most vivid imagination, but despite its summer crowds Cape May almost succeeds in taking one back to the last century. In its older area most of the homes—the tourist folks say about six hundred—have been either well preserved or restored to Victorian splendor with canopied porches, cupolas, widow's walks, and delicately laced woodwork. At night Tiffany lamps shine through leaded windows.

Congress Hall is still there, still laying claim to having been the first summer White House. President Benjamin Harrison kept an office there when he was a guest at the summer home of John Wanamaker, who was Harrison's postmaster general and the founder of the famous Philadelphia department store.

That was in 1890 and '91, and Cape May long before had been calling itself the "Playground of Presidents." Franklin Pierce, Chester Arthur, and Ulysses S. Grant all vacationed there, and Abraham Lincoln spent a few days there while still a Congressman.

The hotel dominates a large beachfront park where John Philip Sousa once led the band concerts and, in fact, premiered a rousing march he entitled "Congress Hall."

Our feathered friends have their own Congress Hall in Cape May—a sort of ornithological Holiday Inn. The Cape is directly under the North American flyway, the birds' I-95 to southern climes, and Roger Tory Peterson, the renowned ornithologist, calls it "one of the country's outstanding bird-watching areas." Peregrine falcons, bald eagles, Cooper's hawks, and ospreys drop in for a short stay at its 181-acre migratory bird refuge, and piping plovers, least and common terns, and yellow warblers breed there.

A couple of hundred years ago whales played off Cape May's beaches, and their taking and rendering was a major occupation until the slaughter drove them off. Now tuna and blues are the game, and Cape May's dredged harbor is headquarters of a large fishing fleet, both commercial and sport.

Here at Cape May is where our voyage North-Northeast begins, a voyage of more than a thousand miles over open ocean, bays, sounds, estuaries, rivers, and even a fjord, past the wide beaches of New Jersey, the skyscraper canyons of New York, the forested hills of Connecticut, the storied coasts of Rhode Island and Massachusetts, the serrated magnificence of Maine.

For our first leg north, it is too bad we can't take the back road up New Jersey's inland waterway, but its waters are too low for our keel and its bridges too low for our mast, and instead of a leisurely trip through almost unspoiled country of cedar and pine and green marsh grass, we must commit to the fickle Atlantic.

11. On the Inlet.

I like to cast off at Cape May in early afternoon, which puts us off Atlantic City about dusk. Just as its gambling towers begin to fade from sight in the gathering darkness astern, we are treated (as we have been several times on previous voyages) to a fireworks display celebrating, I suppose, some sinful accomplishment in those dens of iniquity.

Unless the winds turn foul and the seas go wild, this schedule should put us before dawn close enough, perhaps thirty miles away, to see the glow of New York City. The light of a million street lamps in the city that never sleeps tints the sky above and, on nights when the clouds lie low over the tops of the skyscrapers, sets the overcast itself alight with a phosphorescent loom.

Soon—if we have timed it right, just as we turn the corner of Sandy Hook and head up Ambrose Channel toward New York Harbor—the sun will rise back behind us and extinguish for another day those puny artificial lights which a moment before seemed so bright.

And there ahead of us, suspended on a cushion of morning haze, will be one of the most glorious sights among man's works on earth. Whatever one's impression of New York City from street level, when seen from this vantage point a dozen miles away across the water, with the sun's morning rays sparkling like jewels off its windows and glass buildings, it is magnificent.

We've put behind us a couple of geological features that played important roles in early maritime history. Mount Mitchill, whose 263-foot heighth dominates the Atlantic Highlands, once was the first landfall of most of the sailing vessels approaching the North American continent, and most of them anchored in the bight behind Sandy Hook to replenish their water casks from a bubbling well on the Highlands' slope. The watering hole was marked on charts in Spanish, Portuguese, Dutch, and English, and it was known around the world simply as the "Spout."

The sailor who rounds Sandy Hook for the first time without losing a heartbeat or two has no romance in his soul. Sandy Hook is the hinge to America's front door, gateway to the dreams of Emma Lazarus's huddled masses.

The Statue of Liberty might well have gone here instead of fourteen miles up harbor. For more than a century before Liberty's torch was lighted, the lighthouse at Sandy Hook blinked out a welcome to the arriving millions. Although the shifting sands have left it far back from the beach, the ancient building still stands, the nation's oldest operating lighthouse. It was built by the British, and when they left New York in defeat, they were so certain of an early return that they left its light burning.

Not in operation but almost as old is the Hook's Fort Hancock. When the

12. Coffee Break.

sea was our frontier and the skies did not hold our greatest danger, Fort Hancock was part of our first line of defense.

It was the first of a string of forts built originally to protect New York from the British in the War of 1812. Fort Wadsworth on the Staten Island side and Fort Hamilton on the Brooklyn side of the Narrows were built after that war was over, but on their sites since the days of the Revolution had been artillery batteries behind earthen barricades.

The most important of these batteries were built at the Narrows, that bottleneck where Brooklyn and Staten Island close within a mile of each other before opening out to form New York Harbor. It is crossed now by the Verrazano-Narrows Bridge, which includes the longest suspension span in the world, beating out the best San Francisco's Golden Gate Bridge can do by twenty feet.

13. Fishing Dock.

14. Path to the Point.

15. *South Street Seaport.*

16. *Battery Ferry.*

There at the very base of the great bridge's southern tower, grass and ivy growing through the cracks in its granite face, are the impressive remains of Fort Wadsworth. On the opposite shore, under the north tower but almost lost in the mass of Brooklyn buildings, is still-active Fort Hamilton, now a military headquarters compound.

From their locations artillery batteries, as historian Russell Gilmore puts it, "officially opened and unofficially closed the Revolutionary War."

On the very day the Declaration of Independence was signed, the brash young American artillerymen at what is now Fort Hamilton took a couple of potshots at the British warship *Asia*. His Majesty's ship brought her guns to bear and delivered a broadside that practically wiped out the little battery.

Seven years later, the last cannon shot of the war was fired by a departing British ship in soreheaded pique at a group of jeering American patriots standing on the Staten Island shore.

Those were the last shots ever fired in anger at the Narrows. The British didn't dare try to run the gauntlet of Narrows' batteries in the War of 1812, and by the beginning of World War II the batteries were so heavily armed that they could have delivered one hundred rounds a minute on an enemy ship.

It was across the Narrows that General Howe led his British Redcoats and German mercenaries to attack the upstart Americans in 1776. General Washington's forces were soundly defeated in the Battle of Long Island, but here the general first displayed his military brilliance and conducted the first of what was to be a string of magnificent retreats. The new nation might have ended its days right there if Washington hadn't managed to get most of his army back across the East River to the Manhattan side.

Those forts also played a part in the Civil War, the North using them as prisoner stockades. One of the prisoners was William Henry Fitzhugh Lee, son of the Confederate leader, General Robert E. Lee. Ironically the elder Lee, as a captain almost a quarter of a century before, had supervised the strengthening of the very battlements behind which his son was locked.

Ours is a peaceful passage through the Narrows, our only hazard the big ships that travel this way. While careful navigation is necessary, this isn't the problem it was only a decade or two ago. The harbor of New York that once was one of the world's busiest is a shadow of its former self. Higher labor costs, cargo containerization, shifting population centers, highways, and airplanes all have contributed to the harbor's demise, and today it seems to the casual sailor that there are scarcely more ships using the port than there were back in 1702, when Lord Cornbury reigned as British governor.

Lord Cornbury set a tone that, as far as we know, no New York governor has lived up to since. He was a transvestite who paraded around New York in his wife's dresses.

The sight of miles of abandoned and crumbling docks which so recently bustled with cargo loading or unloading to or from every port of the world is depressing, but it cannot long divert our attention from the grandeur that remains New York Harbor's.

On her tiny island (which itself was once a fort) Liberty continues to reign with new beauty bestowed for her hundredth birthday: her face repainted, her dress redone, her tiara freshly burnished, and her torch restored. And next door on Ellis Island even the shamefully neglected government buildings through which twelve million immigrants passed seeking freedom and fortune in the New World are being spruced up as a more fitting monument to those newcomers' aspirations.

And right across the broad mouth of the Hudson River is the Battery and Manhattan's southern tip. There is no sight like this anywhere in the world, and it must be seen from the deck of a boat. The great steel and concrete and glass spires tower above you, fighting for space as they reach for the heavens.

Floating out on the harbor's dark waters on a crisp fall night, bundled comfortably against the early chill, the sailor gets another privileged view of fairyland. Dusk comes so early that all the offices are still occupied, and their thousands of lights are on. You are close enough so that this great backdrop of light fills your view like a borderless painting. The scene inspires reverential silence.

A little bit of what Manhattan used to be is preserved at the South Street Seaport Museum on the East River almost under the Brooklyn Bridge. Some dedicated maritime preservationists have saved from the wrecker's ball a few blocks of buildings from the early Federal era, and a recent redevelopment of the neighboring and equally historic Fulton Street Fish Market has enhanced the area.

The Seaport's several museum buildings are augmented by two nineteenth-century sailing vessels, the *Wavertree* and the *Peking*. Their tall spars overhead and their bowsprits hanging over the cobbled street below are a small sample of the hundreds of ships that used to crowd rail to rail for most of a mile from the Battery northward.

Wavertree and *Peking* were not among the largest merchantmen that once visited New York, but their size impressed us when we brought *Wyntje* alongside for the first time.

It was a summer day and a goodly crowd of Seaport visitors watched our approach with, I assumed, fascination at seeing a real live sailing vessel coming in

18. Hell Gate.

17. Miss Liberty.

from the sea. I had reckoned with the strong East River current but not with the even stronger eddies along the wharf front itself, and suddenly, as a collective gasp rose from the spectators above, we were being swept down on *Wavertree*.

I gave *Wyntje* the best help her four-cylinder diesel could offer, and we just managed to swing free of the *Wavertree*'s looming hull, but now we were so close that our sixty-four-foot-high mast threatened to crash into the lower of *Wavertree*'s spreading yardarms. With the threatening current and the dock behind me, I had nowhere to go but straight ahead. The flag hoist at the top of our mast just tipped the *Wavertree*'s yardarm with no damage done.

I swung *Wyntje* to the side of the pier, ordered the lines cast ashore, and gave a wave to the crowd, intended as nonchalant affirmation that this was the way we always docked. I hope it was only the sailors among them who could see my heart in my throat.

Traveling up the East River is a whole nautical adventure in itself. For one thing, it is a panorama of modern transportation. We sail under the Brooklyn, Manhattan, Williamsburg, Queensboro, Triborough, Hell Gate, Bronx-Whitestone, and Throgs Neck bridges, the whine of the automobile traffic on the steel grating above providing a deafening ethereal symphonic background for our passage. Subway trains, camouflaged in their graffiti battle paint, rumble overhead, crawling in respect for the age of the bridges and the rails. Helicopters roar away with their commuter traffic from riverside pads at Thirty-fourth and Sixtieth streets. The swaying cars of an overhead tram carry passengers to the big housing development on Roosevelt (nee Blackwell, nee Welfare) Island. Trains carry their intercity passengers and freight across Hell Gate Bridge. Up toward the Long Island end of the river, the big airliners destined to or from La Guardia Airport seem to reach for our mast top as they scream overhead. And most of the way we are accompanied by the cacophony of never-ending traffic on the East River Drive to port.

Back behind that drive stretch the streets of Manhattan. Our water level also is pavement level, and with this peculiar perspective we look down Manhattan's east-west streets. There just beyond the Seaport is New York's first skyscraper, the graceful Gothic Woolworth Building, and behind it the city's currently tallest buildings, the graceless twin slabs of the 110-story (1,350-foot-high) World Trade Center. We pass the vast complex of New York University–Bellevue Medical Center, and down Thirty-fourth Street rises the stately tower of the Empire State Building, long the ruler of this incomparable skyline until the World Trade Center eclipsed it by one hundred feet.

19. New York Harbor.

Down fabled Forty-second Street neither tap dancers nor Times Square are visible from the river, but we can see perhaps the prettiest of the skyscrapers, the stainless steel-clad Art Deco spires of the Chrysler Building.

Now comes into view that repository of man's still-unrealized hope of a peaceful world order, the United Nations; its broad skyscraper administration building and the sweeping parabola housing the General Assembly almost hang above the riverbank.

Next, just beyond the UN, are some of the city's most luxurious apartments, those of Beekman and Sutton places. We have played long-distance Peeping Toms and searched their windows with our binoculars, but we've never seen any of their famed residents such as Greta Garbo or Henry Kissinger peering out. On occasional summer days, however, ladies sunbathing on their terraces have inspired presumably irresistible whistles from our younger crew members.

Sutton Place even features some very fancy town houses whose gardens used to run to the river's bank before master developer Robert Moses laid his East River highway there.

On upstream, past the blocks and blocks of Rockefeller University and adjoining New York Hospital–Cornell University Medical School and Hospital for Special Surgery, is another series of expensive apartments surrounding Gracie Square and the lovely Gracie Mansion, built in 1799 and now the home of New York's mayors.

Over behind us to starboard we have left the industrial waterfront of Brooklyn and Queens with its own point of interest—the Brooklyn Military Ocean Terminal, from which almost five million of America's finest shipped out to save democracy in two world wars. Many heroes had their last view of America there.

And the Brooklyn Navy Yard. It laid down the keel of its first ship of the line, the seventy-four-gun USS *Ohio*, in 1817, and 125 years later, during World War II, it was still building, repairing, and servicing much of the Atlantic fleet. Now the historic old yard, like so much of the Brooklyn waterfront, is virtually deserted.

We have made our way up the East River with the current. It is the only way to go. The water runs at up to four knots through here, and it can be a slow passage against it—slow and dangerous. Although the Coast Guard does a valiant job with its large floating "vacuum cleaners" to keep the river clean, it is regularly awash with huge timbers that break off from the decaying docks. Waterlogged, they float frequently just below the surface. If a small vessel meets them at any speed disaster can result, but fatal consequences are far more likely if one meets them head-on as they come sweeping down with the tide.

20. East Side in Rain.

ONE
FRESH FRUIT VEGETABLES

21. *Antique Shop.*

Just opposite Gracie Mansion, where the Harlem and East rivers join, those fierce currents make up into the treacherous opening called, for good reason, Hell Gate. They tumble and swirl and occasionally form such whirlpools that they can overwhelm a helmsman and capsize a good-sized vessel.

Sailing vessels and the bones of their hapless crews litter the bottom of the river there, but even powerful modern ships have lost to their fury. Only a few years ago, a tugboat was swept below and her crew joined the other Hell Gate victims.

Unless the captain times his passage to make it at slack, sailing through the Gate always is a thrill. The current drags at the rudder, the wheel in your hands tugs one way and then another, the bow swings out of path, and like driving a race car around a curve, there is the feeling that you are sailing on the very edge of disaster.

Through Hell Gate and under the Triborough and railway bridges and one has a wider and calmer path for the short run to Long Island Sound. We pass the huge Consolidated Edison power plant (for obscure reasons affectionately known by New Yorkers as "Big Alice") and we are at Rikers Island, on which is crowded the New York City prison.

Across from it, on our port, is North Brother Island, with its abandoned isolation hospital to which those with communicable diseases were banished before the miracles of modern medicine. The hospital ruins are an unintended memorial to the East River's worst disaster, for it was here on June 15, 1904, that the burning excursion steamer, the *General Slocum*, was run aground as 1,031 lives were lost, most of them women and children on a church picnic.

We sail on past La Guardia Field, and we are at Throgs Neck and the twin forts which once guarded the passage between the sound and the East River route to Manhattan.

Fort Schuyler on our port is now the home of the State University of New York Maritime College, and it is particularly worthy today of at least one note: In a prize-winning conversion (that one would like to think was symbolic), architect William A. Hall turned the casemates where the great guns once were lodged into a library.

Opposite Schuyler is abandoned Fort Totten, which at the turn of this century served as antisubmarine headquarters and as late as World War II was antiaircraft headquarters for the Eastern Defense Command.

Much of our early American history was written on the waters of Long Island Sound. This inland sea is ninety miles long and up to twenty miles across, and today it is one of the world's great recreational boating areas. Authorities figure very roughly that three hundred thousand boats make their home in the sound's scores of marinas and clubs, and by far the largest part of them are in that half of the sound west of Stratford Shoal. Here on any given Sunday in summer it seems that they all are out, everything from rowboats to princely yachts, in a chaos of patternless traffic.

Contretemps are as inevitable as on any crowded freeway. There is at least one recorded case of an indignant fisherman who threw crankcase oil over the sail of a yacht that had cut his line. It is a wonder that more serious combat has not erupted. Like opposing nations at war, both racing sailors and fishermen pray to the same God and both believe He has given them rights to the same spot of water. Happily, shouted deprecations usually to the moment suffice.

Hempstead and Huntington harbors and Oyster Bay and Port Jefferson on the Long Island side and Mamaroneck, Stamford, and Norwalk on the Connecticut side are the largest centers of all this activity, but the queen of them all is venerable City Island. It was a yachting center long before cheap plastics and greater leisure time brought the post-World War II boating boom and before New York City spread its suburban tentacles out along the shoreline.

22. *Little Harbor.*

23. *Old Water Tower.*

24. Fall at Cold Spring.

25. *The Bell.*

Politically this twenty-four-block-long, one- to four-block-wide island belongs to New York City, an exotic northern outpost of the Bronx. But spiritually it belongs to the sea and to another age. Until developers discovered it just a few years ago its neat, middle-class clapboard houses were peopled by those who, as their fathers before them, worked in the boatyards and sail lofts that lined the main street.

Here at yards like Minnefords and Nevins were built many of this century's most famous pleasure and racing yachts. Minnefords itself built four of the vessels that defended the America's Cup.

It was out of City Island Yacht Club that in my earliest sailing days I made my first tentative forays into Long Island Sound: first, just the mile or so out to Stepping Stones Light, and then a mile or so farther to Execution Rocks, so named by the colonials who dispatched their capital offenders there.

I made all the mistakes in the book, and some not there. Misfiguring the tide and the abating wind, I bounced on the rocks of nearby Hart Island, fearing for the moment that I might join there the uncounted thousands laid in paupers' graves over the last century. On more than one occasion I missed my mooring under sail and, fighting to regain control, ricocheted through the anchored fleet at the club as celebrating members, home from the weekend's races, dropped their drinks and hastened to defend their topsides.

Among those early adventures was my first "long distance" voyage, all of thirteen miles to Greenwich. I spent days planning the trip—food, bedding for the night I would be anchored in Greenwich Harbor, a detailed buoy-by-buoy plot of my course. It turned out it was well that I had taken the latter precaution. The sail up was in a heavy haze, and I could barely see the next buoy ahead. When Greenwich appeared dead ahead through the haze, I dubbed myself Cronkite the Navigator.

The next day, however, the wind had gone northwest and it was breathtakingly clear. As I sailed around the corner of Great Captain Island that guards Greenwich Harbor, chart in hand to find my way home, there looming on the horizon in front of me was the skyline of Manhattan and, sharply delineated, was almost every buoy and rock all the way to City Island. Commodore Walter Mitty stripped Cronkite the Navigator of his buttons.

That summer haze is not an infrequent condition on the sound and through history has shrouded from time to time bloody, nefarious, and heroic goings-on. The earliest colonists depended on their small boats to trade from settlement to settlement, and these often were intercepted by piratical Indians who killed the crews, plundered the cargoes, and seized the boats for further depredations.

26. *Napping.*

28. Mist at Eatons Neck.

27. Winter . . . Lloyd Neck.

29. *The Boathouse.*

30. *Mussel Pickers.*

31. *Walking the Flats.*

32. *Seawanhaka Yacht Club.*

33. *First Snow.*

34. *Harbor Roses.*

35. Montauk Light.

36. Beach Walker.

These Indians met their match, however, when they ran into a Mr. Tilley who, according to historian Horace Beck, was "known as Sergeant Kettle because he wore a brass pot on his head in battle." Mr. Tilley may have invented the modern helmet, but it failed to save him the day he was loading hay at Six Mile Island (now known as Nott Island). He and his crew were ambushed and roasted alive.

During the Revolution and again in the War of 1812 the Americans, under cover of haze, fog, or night, slipped out of hiding places along the Connecticut shore, notably the Norwalk Islands, to raid the British on Long Island.

On a hill near Setauket on Long Island, Ann Strong, a member of the Culper ring of Revolutionaries, signalled the colonial whaleboats when it was safe to land. She used her wash line. If the message, for instance, was that the British would not come for two hours, she might hang one set of red long johns and two white handkerchiefs. She varied the articles of clothing and their colors to improvise a code that the U.S. Signal Corps might envy.

It was near there, at Huntington, that Captain Nathan Hale landed by sloop from Norwalk to spy on the British. He was caught and hanged and on the gibbet uttered the words that assured him a place in history: "I only regret that I have but one life to lose for my country."

One hundred and fifty years later there were other strange nocturnal doings in the coves of the Long Island shore. This was a natural center of prohibition rum-running. Fast, onetime World War I gunboats, now invariably painted black to avoid detection, sped the illicit cargo from freighters lying offshore to beachside rendezvous from which trucks took it on to slake the nation's thirst.

There were occasional outbursts of gang warfare, shootings, and hijackings on the beaches and roads of then-sparsely settled Long Island, but it was not that which bothered the residents so much. The traffic of the bootleg trucks was so heavy that their more frequent complaint was of the nighttime noise.

Some of the estate owners did note on occasion, however, their annoyance when they would find the otherwise pristine sand of their private beaches cut up by the tracks of beached boats and heavy trucks.

Sailing down Long Island Sound is like voyaging through the pages of *Who's Who*.

Those grand buildings over there at Kings Point off the starboard bow as you sail out into the sound from the East River, over there where all the flags are, where the United States Merchant Marine Academy is now, that used to be the estate of Walter Chrysler, the auto king.

37. Sunlit Beach.

A little farther along are the mansions of the late John Hay Whitney, Otto Kahn, Harrison Williams, Marshall Field, and William K. Vanderbilt, and around the corner at Glen Cove, Long Island, financier J. P. Morgan docked his *Corsair*, the grandest yacht of the many grand yachts that once ran their owners in luxury down the East River to Wall Street in the morning and home in the evening. Now helicopters and seaplanes make this plush commuting run from the millionaires' estates that still dot Long Island's North Shore.

This area was once so resolutely insular in its exclusivity that its socialite residents even developed their own speech pattern, affected by both sexes but particularly favored by the female of the species. It is practised by speaking with the lips as nearly closed as possible. It can be heard today and is referred to by students of such matters as "Long Island Lockjaw," or, delineating the locale more specifically, "Locust Valley Lockjaw."

Sagamore Hill, which dominates Oyster Bay a bit farther east of Glen Cove, of course was Teddy Roosevelt's beloved home. He rowed the bay's waters with bully enthusiasm and with Mrs. Roosevelt, we are told, as a willing passenger. There is no record that she shared with him an enthusiasm for sailing, a curse visited upon not a few men besides our twenty-sixth president.

This determinedly rustic house of Roosevelt's in the lovely quiet of its tree-rimmed setting seems an unlikely place to stop a war, but there the president

38. Sag Harbor Yacht Club.

negotiated the agreement that, signed shortly thereafter at Portsmouth, New Hampshire, brought an end to the Russo-Japanese conflict. Roosevelt won the Nobel Peace Prize for that.

He shared Oyster Bay with the avid sailors of Seawanhaka Corinthian Yacht Club, one of the nation's oldest yacht clubs and certainly one of the finest on the North Shore. There are not many of the great East Coast yachtsmen who have not picked up its moorings and lifted a cooling drink on its broad veranda.

Directly across the sound, Connecticut boasts its own gold coast of great estates perched royally behind its rocky shore. W. T. Grant, founder of the dollar store chain (that's when a dollar *was* a dollar, young man!), built the big place on the port side as you sail into Greenwich, and right around the corner you pass the gracious home of Victor Borge, with its huge lawn sweeping down to the water's edge. Victor once remarked that it took half of the proceeds from his highly successful concerts just to pay his gardener.

As you head up toward the Indian Harbor Yacht Club, whose big stucco building dominates the harbor, over to starboard and just beyond the club is the mansion where local legend stoutly maintains that Grover Cleveland had his secret cancer operation in 1893. Actually that successful operation to remove a malignancy from the president's mouth took place on *Oneida*, Commodore Elias C. Benedict's splendid yacht that, indeed, was based in Greenwich but at the time of the surgery was cruising languidly out of reporters' prying reach somewhere on Long Island Sound.

The post-World War II megapolitan spread out from New York has engulfed most of the Long Island Sound shore, and housing developments, cheek-to-jowl marinas, industry, and oil depots have changed the character of many of the once-unique harbors, but there remain fascinating cul-de-sacs along the ragged coastline.

In Oyster Bay, anchor at dusk in the shadow under Sagamore Hill and at dawn take the dinghy in to Cold Spring Harbor. Back up the road it is a busy suburban city with all the used-car lots and shopping centers that implies, but down at the waterfront it isn't all that much changed from its whaling days, the old inn still doing business and another generation of kids and older folks tumbling into rowboats for a morning of fishing.

Cross the sound to Connecticut. At Stratford feel your way up the narrow and shallow river a mile or so, anchor there on the edge of the tall marsh grass, and in the evening attend the unique Shakespeare Theater with its troubadours who stroll the picnic gardens before the night's performance. (You can do all that if the theater is open—it lately has suffered financial problems.)

39. Montauk Dunes.

Farther on, the Thimble Islands give the Long Island Sound sailor a taste of Maine. Two dozen islands, each large enough for at least one house and a handsome copse of pines and firs, huddle together in the lee of the Connecticut shore with just enough room for boats to squeeze between or anchor for the night.

The Connecticut River, which opens into the sound toward its eastern end, is one of the country's great ecological and historical treasures. Its waters that course down from Canada and most of the New England states supply almost half the sound's fresh water, and their meeting with the salt water coming in from the ocean has created a great salt-fresh-brackish estuary that is a fish-and-bird nursery of inestimable value. Uncommon and endangered species have found sanctuary in its protected marshes: the bald eagle and American bittern, the Atlantic salmon and shortnose sturgeon among them.

Here at the Connecticut's mouth is the only town I know of that was named for settlers who never kept their date with destiny. Back in the early 1600s, a likely spot at the broad entrance to the river was prepared as a place of refuge for Lord Saye and Lord Brooke, who were among the Parliamentarians annoying Charles I with their persistence in seeking constitutional rights. But with the Cromwellian revolution, Saye and Brooke decided they didn't need to flee to America.

"Why should we go through all that colonial bother now?" they might well have asked. "After all, we've already got the town named after us."

So they did, and it has been Saybrook ever since.

Past the broad marshes of the estuary the Connecticut narrows to wind between forested bluffs, and there as the narrowing begins is Essex, rich in history and a perfect jewel of a preserved colonial city. Up the hill that rises swiftly from the docks great maples, lindens, and evergreens spread their mantles over Main Street and its colonial houses, the whole given even greater authenticity by the continued presence of the gracious old Griswold Inn, opened in 1776 and continuing to do business.

There are two more rivers to explore before Connecticut runs into Rhode Island at Stonington, itself a pretty and historic town, historic if for no other reason than it once was the southern terminus of the railroad from Boston and hence a major transshipping center for the important New York trade.

The Thames River is notable for the fact that we colonials always have defied our British cousins by rhyming it with rain, plains, and Spain instead of with Ben, as in Big Ben, as they do.

The Thames also is notable for harboring a startling anachronism. As you sail up its broad reaches, over to port at the Coast Guard Academy may well be docked the United States armed services' only active sailing ship, the beautiful

40. Coming Ashore.

three-masted *Eagle*, while over to starboard at General Dynamics' vast submarine factory almost certainly will be docked the latest of our most modern nuclear submarines.

Around the corner from New London, up through the treacherously rock-studded Fishers Island Sound, is the almost-hidden entrance to the comparatively short Mystic River. At its head, barely three miles from the mouth, is the exciting Mystic Seaport Museum, an authentic re-creation of a mid-nineteenth-century whaling village.

Most sailors are romantics, and to sail into Mystic Seaport as the sun begins to set behind the trees that shade the lovely colonial houses on the far shore is one of the most romantic of experiences.

The sun bounces golden off the tall masts of the old whaling ship *Charles W. Morgan*, restored and laying to her stone pier as if waiting for her captain to order another sailing for distant seas. You maneuver in just behind her and warp to a dock from which you can step ashore into another century.

Along the cobblestoned wharf you stride past the blacksmith shop, the barrel maker's, and the printer's to the sail loft and beyond to the old shipyard, where Mystic's fleet of preserved sailing vessels is repaired with the tools and skills of olden days.

And retracing your steps you come back by way of the village's main dirt street, past the dry goods store, the church, and the old pharmacy.

Tied up there at night, the crowd of visitors gone and peace and quiet descended, you share the gathering dark with the ghosts of seafaring generations past. It is an incomparable experience.

Sailing back down the Mystic River and following the channel's tricky turns through an expanse of shallow water, I am reminded of the time a boatload of young people sped past us here, its occupants shouting and waving their arms. I waved back a cheery greeting and my faithful mate said, "What do you think they were shouting?"

"Why, 'Hello, Walter,' " I replied.

"No," she said. "They were shouting, 'Low water.' "

Such are the pitfalls of fame's egotism.

Back across Fishers Island Sound and past the huge mansions of Fishers Island itself, we sail through the Race, the turbulent corridor where Long Island Sound flows out to Block Island Sound and the Atlantic beyond. We set a course south for the Long Island shore and Shelter Island.

A twelve-square-mile colony of summer homes, Shelter Island is cradled in a curved palm of Long Island, and it invites circumnavigation not only because of the beauty of the passage but also because behind it lies one of the most interesting of all the area's colonial towns, Sag Harbor.

It was a British bastion in the Revolutionary War and the scene of an audacious attack by raiding colonists, it was an American fort and arsenal in the War of 1812 and a base for daring attacks on the British fleet that stood outside, and it was a major port while whaling was in favor.

Remnants of its lush history dot the village, including the cemetery where many of Captain David Hand's wives are buried. The captain was one of the few whalers who survived that dangerous occupation into old age, and he laid away seven or eight wives who did not survive him. He buried them in a row in the cemetery and, the story goes, as he made his way to the docks each morning, he would doff his hat to each of them in turn with a solemn greeting: "Good morning, Susannah; good morning, Mary; . . . "

If town historian George Finckenor is to be believed, and I certainly don't doubt him, Sag Harbor continues today to contribute folk stories to our history. George Balanchine, the great ballet choreographer, is buried in Oakland Cemetery there. On occasional days not otherwise celebrated, a large black limousine drives up. A woman gets out. She is slight with muscular legs and dressed in black, her face hidden by a heavy veil. She walks quickly to the grave, lays flowers on it, stands with her head bowed for a minute, and leaves. Balanchine has become to Sag Harbor's Oakland what Rudolph Valentino was to Hollywood's Memorial Park Cemetery.

Sag Harbor has a special place in my memory, a recollection of the day that, caught in a sudden and severe nor'easter, I found refuge there and, having radioed ahead, was met by my good friend the late John Steinbeck, waiting at the dock, wind whipped and rain soaked, ready to give me a hand with the lines.

John sailed those waters with me, full as always of the region's lore, particularly that of Gardiners Island, which lies just off the Long Island shore from Sag Harbor. Surely Gardiners is one of the most fascinating pieces of real estate in all the world.

It is the only estate on the North American continent that is in the fourth century of continuous ownership under the same name. The deed is now held by Robert D. L. Gardiner. His ancestor Lion Gardiner, who had built the fortifications against the Dutch along the Connecticut River, originally bought the land from the Indians in 1639, and then he secured his rights to the property by buying a supplementary deed from Charles I for five pounds.

The island is just under four thousand acres, twenty-seven miles around the frequently rocky, sometimes sandy beach. Gardiners and their servants fought off

Indian raids in the early days and, in 1728, repulsed an attack by Spanish pirates which left the manor house in ruins.

By the time of the Revolution the Gardiners were skilled at survival, and they supported both the patriots and the British. In the War of 1812, the British fleet anchored off the island, and its officers were entertained at sumptuous banquets ashore while the Gardiners resupplied the vessels that went on to land the troops that burned Washington.

Long before the Revolution, in the late seventeenth century, the Gardiners and the William Kidd family were good friends with neighboring town houses on Beaver Street in Manhattan. After Kidd took to piracy, he continued to visit his friend's island, and the only authenticated burial place of his ill-gotten treasure was there.

He buried near Cherry Hill twenty-four chests loaded with diamonds, rubies, gold bars, silver, pearls, and East Indian brocades with real gold thread shot through the silk, an Indian mogul's dowry for his daughter. Sailing away he told John, third lord of the manor, "If I come back and the treasure isn't here, I shall have your head or your son's."

Kidd was caught and hanged shortly after, and the treasure was recovered by crown agents. Lord Bellomont gave John Gardiner a detailed receipt for the loot. Two hundred and sixty years later, in 1959, Robert Gardiner received a copy of the receipt the royal household gave to Bellomont when he turned the treasure over to the crown. It was minus six diamonds, which Robert Gardiner assumes Bellomont snitched.

Robert's great-aunt Julia set her cap for the bachelor President John Tyler. Her father, who was a senator, invited her to join the exclusive party on the USS *Princeton*, where the president was to view the firing before Mount Vernon of the biggest gun yet built by the navy. (Shades of a later day, it was called the "Peacemaker.") Just before the firing, Julia feigned faintness and asked the president to join her below for a glass of champagne. They were there when the gun backfired, killing the secretaries of army and navy and Julia's father.

"She literally stepped over her father's body into the White House," Robert Gardiner cheerfully recounts, for she went on to marry Tyler and become a powerful influence in Washington, persuading her husband to annex Texas and introducing "Hail to the Chief" as the president's musical signature.

Gardiners Island today boasts a thirty-eight-room manor house, its fourth; 1,250 acres of virgin oak forest; twenty miles of road; an airport; its own power supply replenished by tanker once a year; and a working windmill, the last of five which once graced the fiefdom.

41. Beached Schooner.

42. The Harbor Light.

It is home to six hundred swans, six hundred Canadian geese, some one thousand wild turkeys, and so many deer that three hundred have to be shot each year to prevent their starvation. Gardiner, proud that he has maintained the family fortune through shrewd investment, lives most of the time on the mainland in nearby East Hampton, in the home that was John Tyler's summer White House in Julia's day.

Sail east-northeast from Gardiners Island twenty-five miles along the fast-fading Long Island shore and you come upon a quite different island, named for himself in 1614 by the Dutch explorer Adriaen Block.

Incidentally, Block built his sixteen-ton ship, *Onrust*, on the Manhattan site where, a hundred years later and after some landfill, a black West Indian named Samuel Fraunces would establish the tavern which hosted George Washington's farewell to his troops at the end of the Revolutionary War.

Block Island is a delightfully wild place of steep hills and flower-covered moors dotted with the homes of summer residents. It rises in the south to drop suddenly into the Atlantic, the two-hundred-foot-high bluffs reminding the approaching sailor of the cliffs of Dover. Its broad, protected Great Salt Pond is a popular rendezvous of sailing craft and sleek sportfishing boats that hunt big game—swordfish, tuna, marlin, and sharks—far out to sea.

Once a year it is the scene of Block Island Race Week, which attracts hundreds of sailors for spirited racing and even more spirited hijinks in the broad-verandaed old resort hotels and seafood restaurants ashore.

These are some of the most famous sailboat-racing waters in the world, for it is in the broad Rhode Island Sound between Block Island Sound and Narragansett Bay that the America's Cup was defended every three years from 1958 until the Australians took it home with them in 1983.

The base for those races, of course, was Newport, America's first resort. Its usually pleasant summer climate was "discovered" early in the nineteenth century by Southerners who brought first their cotton to its busy port and later their families for the season. The Civil War ended all that, but toward the end of the century, New York society found the place and built the spectacular mansions they demurely called "cottages."

Far into this century it was popular to call New York's most privileged society the "Four Hundred," for that is the number that Mrs. Astor believed her ballroom would hold. In recent years that limit has been considerably exceeded by those who rent Newport's grand mansions for various entertainments during the America's Cup races.

The Newport Restoration Foundation claims that Newport has more original colonial homes than any other place in the United States, and thanks to valiant

43. Harbor Road.

restoration efforts led by tobacco heiress Doris Duke over the last decade, the narrow streets running up the hill behind Newport's busy waterfront today are a living and colorful museum of pastel-shaded houses with gambrel roofs.

Sailors of all the seagoing nations have trod those streets in centuries past, and even among this generation of the world's racing sailors there probably is no waterfront street any better known than Newport's Thames Street, with its jumble of boatyards, chandleries, fish wharves, hotels, and bars—particularly bars.

44. *Painting the Hull.*

At least one tavern operating today on Thames Street has known the boots of pirates, privateers, whalers, and merchantmen, and there is the printing establishment founded by Ben Franklin's brother, a headstone-carving shop which has been in continuous operation at the same location since 1705, and Trinity Church at which George Washington worshipped.

Up the bay a piece from Newport, at Bristol, is the boatyard where the justly famed Herreshoffs thrived.

The blind John Brown Herreshoff founded the yard to exploit the brilliant designs of his brother, Nathanael Greene Herreshoff, an engineering graduate of Massachusetts Institute of Technology. They built everything from the first U.S. Navy torpedo boats to eight successful defenders of the America's Cup, and their work was admired around the world.

Several recent America's Cup contenders have come from the modern Newport yard of Williams & Manchester. The Herreshoffs, the Saunders family across the bay, and others were the progenitors of an industry on Narragansett Bay that today is turning out a large percentage of this nation's pleasure craft.

As we sail out of Newport Harbor to continue our northeast voyage, we pass to port Hammersmith Farm, a notable landmark. Its sprawling white mansion sits at the crown of a great lawn, part of the landscaping designed by the man who laid out New York's Central Park, Frederick Law Olmsted. Then-owner of Hammersmith, Mrs. Hugh Auchincloss, held the reception there when her daughter Jackie married Senator John Fitzgerald Kennedy.

45. *Block Island Ruins.*

46. North Point Light.

47. *Ida Lewis Yacht Club.*

48. *The Black Pearl.*

49. In From the Fog.

Here begins the rock-rimmed New England Coast that continues with rare exception beyond the Canadian border, and we must navigate carefully to avoid Brenton Reef, the first of many submerged outcroppings that from now on threaten the unwary mariner.

Reefs named Hen and Chickens, Old Cock, and the Wildcat lie ahead, but we'll leave them well abeam as we make for one of our favorite anchorages, Cuttyhunk Island. A gentle southwesterly, the prevailing wind for summer, boosts us along, and the island will appear shortly through the haze, not a half-day's sail away.

It is well we will reach there early to get the hook down or pick up one of the town's moorings. In summer the little keyhole harbor fills early, sailboats at the deeper end, sportfishermen around the dock at the other.

Cuttyhunk is a cute little nub of a place, essentially one small 150-foot hill on which a few families live year round, joined each year by a handful of summer people. There isn't much to do, but perhaps that is the point. And anyway, the view from the hilltop is spectacular.

This really is the gateway to a vast 1,800-square-mile vacationland that includes Cape Cod; Martha's Vineyard; Nantucket; mainland communities like Dartmouth, Mattapoisett, and Marion; and the waters of Buzzards Bay and Vineyard and Nantucket sounds that lie in between.

Martha's Vineyard at its nearest point is just four miles off Cape Cod, but it is a world unto itself. Packed into its 108 square miles is incredible topographical, social, and economic variety. Its Vineyard Sound shore is rocky, forested, and framed by bluffs, the spectacular multicolored clay bluffs of Gay Head at the western end. On the Atlantic side there are bluffs too, but mostly miles of wide, soft beaches and great dunes of sand. Inland there are flat lands of lush farms; ragged, windswept hills; ponds rich in clams and mussels, crabs, eels, snapping turtles; and flocks of ducks and geese feeding on an abundance of wild celery and wild rice.

Its towns are as varied as its land. Edgartown is its showplace, an almost perfectly preserved town of the eighteenth and nineteenth centuries. Once a whaling port, the stately captains' houses continue to stand in their white-uniformed grandeur along its treelined waterfront.

50. Fishing the Surf.

Oak Bluffs has its own claim on the visitor's attention. Back in the middle of the last century, a Methodist Meeting Ground was built there. A great cone-shaped tabernacle is at its center and around it, so close together a man can scarcely pass between them, are tiny Victorian cottages, each a gingerbread fantasy.

Most of the village of Vineyard Haven's architectural heritage went up in flames in the great fire of 1883, but the rebuilt town is the island's largest and its commercial hub.

I've always thought Martha's Vineyard deserved more recognition by the cosmetic industry as the possible birthplace of suntan lotion. An early historian noted that the skin of the Indians there was "olive or copper in color, not so much by the science of nature as by the constant application of oil and grease and exposure to the elements."

It was to Martha's Vineyard that Joshua Slocum came in 1902 to retire just four years after completing his famous voyage, the first time anyone had sailed alone around the world.

He chose a farm in West Tisbury, in the island's heart, about as far from the sea as one can get there. His neighbors were other retired sea captains, and it is both a tribute to the island's beauty and a comment on a man's sentiments after a life at sea that so many of them would choose West Tisbury's lovely rolling hills rather than an ocean view.

Slocum kept his equally famous little thirty-seven-foot sloop *Spray* in the nearby fishing harbor of Menemsha, but apparently neither he nor it made much of a splash on the Vineyard. The *Vineyard Gazette* noticed that Slocum had taken up residence with but two sentences, and Captain Donald LeMar Poole, himself an almost legendary fisherman, told an interviewer years later that "not much fuss was made here over Slocum." Poole attributed part of that at least to the fact that Slocum was a merchantman and most of his neighbors had been whalers, and there wasn't much love lost between the two groups.

Perhaps even more important was the simple fact that Slocum was an off-islander. It seems to be a hallmark of New England's island people, perhaps born of a healthy sense of their own permanence of self and place, that they are somewhat suspicious of the transient fame of those who increasingly come to live among them for at least a few months a year.

On the Vineyard Beverly Sills, Art Buchwald, Bill Styron, John Hersey, John Marquand, Jr., Mike Wallace, Carly Simon, Garson Kanin, Robert McNamara, Cyrus Vance, Kay Graham, Ed Bennett Williams get no more than the same polite nod from their neighbors and the same cheerful dilatory service from carpenters, painters, and plumbers as the rest of the residents.

51. Beached Dinghies.

This admirable, if unique, sense of values appears in unexpected ways.

At Siasconset, the beautiful village of rose-covered onetime fishermen's cottages on Nantucket's eastern bluffs, the trashman for many years was a courtly Yankee gentleman who bore the good pioneer Nantucket name of Coffin. One morning as on his calls he was having his regular cup of coffee with Marjorie Benchley, wife of the late novelist Nathaniel Benchley, she said to him, "Mr. Coffin, you've known our family so long, why don't you call me 'Marjorie?' "

Drawing himself up to his full dignity, Mr. Coffin replied, "Nevah."

Nantucket's character is vastly different from the Vineyard's. It is more of an "island" island. Smaller than its neighbor eighteen miles away and considerably farther out to sea, it is more unidimensional: flatter, sandier, foggier, and perhaps, for all those reasons, more romantic.

Its major town is also called Nantucket, and befitting its position as once the nation's major whaling port, its captains' houses are made of brick, and they are grandly situated on the hill behind the harbor at the end of cobblestoned Main Street.

To the anguish of conservationists, the town's ramshackle waterfront was rebuilt a few years ago with a modern marina, shops, and restaurants. But the nineteenth-century style of a New England fishing village was retained, and today the area is a major tourist attraction.

I never sail around the Brant Point Lighthouse guarding the entrance to Nantucket's inner harbor that I don't tip my cap to the ingenuity of our forefathers. Under us there lies a sandbar that should have kept Nantucket from ever becoming the great whaling port it was.

What those old boys did almost two hundred years ago was simply invent a device to lift the heavy whalers over the bar. Called a "camel," it was a huge wooden dry dock built in two pieces. It was sunk, fitted around the whaler, the water pumped out, and whaler and camel were then towed across the bar.

The device kept Nantucket at the top of the whaling business until the whalers, depleting nearby resources, had to go farther and farther to find their prey. Then they needed larger ships, and the larger ships needed a deeper harbor. Thus came New Bedford's moment in the whaling sun.

New Bedford is only eight to ten hours or so by whaler from Nantucket—over on the mainland side of Buzzards Bay. Seldom thought of as a tourist mecca today, New Bedford nonetheless to a sea-loving person is one of the most interesting cities on our northeastern coast.

52. Flower Cart.

53. Morning Haze.

54. *Heading Out.*

55. *Gathering Butterfly Weed.*

56. Kingdom by the Sea.

57. Underweigh at Dawn.

58. The Potting Shed.

59. Edgartown Departure.

60. *After Colors.*

61. *Island Morning.*

62. Park Street Church.

Its fishing fleet, so troubled in recent years by foreign incursions into waters off the North American shores and the resultant overfishing, today consists of some 225 vessels, each worth up to a million dollars or more, and together employing fifteen hundred to two thousand stalwart men, many of Portuguese ancestry.

When New Bedford was the nation's largest whaling port in the middle of the last century, more than three hundred whaling ships were registered there shipping aboard ten thousand men. The city was said to be the nation's richest per capita and its fourth busiest port.

The decline of whaling began in 1859 with Drake's discovery of oil in Pennsylvania, and the last whaler sailed out of New Bedford in 1925. The decline was speeded during the Civil War when the North bought up the whaling ships, filled them with stones, and sank them to blockade Charleston Harbor.

In its whaling heyday the city, believe it or not, was infested with Pacific Islands cannibals and headhunters. They were inexperienced hands shanghaied by desperate whaling captains who, once safely back home in New Bedford, dumped them ashore.

They inhabited an area known as Hard Dig, a mean, bad, colorful area. And the center of Hard Dig was, what else, a beached whaling ship. It became a bar and brothel called the Ark, the nameplate having been taken off a ship that was being broken up after serving her time faithfully as a legitimate whaler out of Nantucket.

Irate citizens later torched her; the fire almost got out of control and led to the creation of the New Bedford Fire Department, bestowing a unique birthright on that sterling body.

One of the rare occupations of these stranded South Sea Islanders was the sale of shrunken heads, some of which it was said were real but many of which were counterfeit, realistically fashioned out of coconut and rope.

It was in New Bedford that Frederick Douglass lived his first three years as a free man and began to establish his reputation as a great lecturer and newspaper publisher.

And among its prominent residents was the wealthy merchant Samuel Rodman who, among other things, distinguished himself by writing that he didn't think much of young Congressman Abraham Lincoln as a public speaker.

Rodman was one of the nation's early weathermen, albeit amateur. He took weather readings three times a day for thirty years, compiling the country's oldest continuous weather records.

63. *The Moors.*

64. *Siasconset Lane.*

65. Nantucket Basket.

New Bedford's twin city of Fall River also had its place in maritime history as the terminus of the famous Fall River Steamship Line. In the days when railroad travel was still plagued by smoke, cinders, and a lack of air-conditioning, travel by boat was far more comfortable, and the line carried almost half a million passengers a year between New York and Massachusetts.

They traveled in considerable luxury. The great side-wheeler *Commonwealth*, which operated right up until the eve of World War II, was described by the *Vineyard Gazette* at her launching in 1907 as having "a two-deck Venetian-Gothic saloon, a mahogany-and-gold Empire saloon, and marvel of marvels, an English Renaissance Café high up against the skyline."

One could board the *Commonwealth* or one of her sister ships, the *Plymouth*, *Providence*, and *Priscilla*, at New York's Pier 14 in the evening after work; sail up the East River in the sunset; have a good meal and a night's sleep; and after transferring to the fast train at Fall River in the morning, be in Boston at 8:40 A.M. What a way to go!

The depression and a seamen's strike forced the folding of the Fall River Line in 1937, and when the great side-wheelers were towed down Narragansett Bay to be broken up in a Baltimore yard, thousands of people lined the shore to bid them, and an era of our maritime history, farewell.

The *Priscilla*'s big steam whistle, an ornately carved newel-post from her grand stairway, and a red plush settee from the main saloon are in the Marine Museum at Fall River, hard by the old Fall River dock and train station.

The steamers of the Fall River Line shared the waters of Buzzards Bay and Vineyard and Nantucket sounds with the great four-, five-, and even six-masted schooners that also carried a heavy portion of the coal and timber that moved along our coast right up until the mid-twenties of this century.

They were the last in the great parade of shipping that had grown continuously since the days when romantically named Tarpaulin Cove on Naushon Island was the lair of pirates such as Captain Kidd and Thomas Pound. To guide this commerce through the treacherous waters of Vineyard and Nantucket sounds, some of the colonies' first lighthouses were erected here—Tarpaulin Cove's light in 1759 and Gay Head's in 1799.

Before the building of the Cape Cod Canal, one of the most dangerous parts of their passage was through the swift currents of shoal-ridden Nantucket Sound. The tidal rips around the northeast corner of the Vineyard, an area well-named West Chop, are fearsome. When a strong wind, particularly a nor'easter, runs against the three-and-a-half-knot current, the water boils, and right between the Vineyard and Nobska Point on Cape Cod there sits a four-foot spot called the Middle Ground, ready to catch the errant, unwary, or unlucky skipper.

Some Higher Authority with more experience as a skipper than mine must have been watching over me when I first sailed these waters. One lazy day, probably more interested in my guests' conversation than my navigation, I suddenly found that the swift currents had carried us directly over the Middle Ground, and *Wyntje* was saved only by the good grace of it being high tide.

I also have been almost trapped by Horseshoe Shoal, one of the many shallow spots that make of Nantucket Sound a labyrinth not to be assayed by the unskilled sailor in a deep-draft boat. On a hazy day, I lost sight of the buoys and lost track of the current and found the bottom rising to meet the keel. I headed in every direction of the compass to find deep water and was despairing of salvation when the Fathometer at last started climbing, and we knew we had broken through.

Fortunately it was a calm day, but I thought of what that predicament could have meant if the wind had been piping up and if we had not had an engine to back up the sails. Not so many decades ago and under just slightly less favorable conditions, Horseshoe would have claimed another victim.

Indeed the records show that in the age of sail, scores of vessels were wrecked each year on Horseshoe, L'Hommedieu Shoal, Hedge Fence, Bishop and Clerks, Halfmoon Shoal, Cross Rip Shoal, the aptly named Wreck Shoal, and the huge complex of sandbars collectively known as Monomoy Shoals, which guard the eastern entrance to the sound and in the distant geologic past undoubtedly formed a continuous landmass from Cape Cod across Monomoy Island to Nantucket.

On one of the area's many sparkling summer days, to the casual layman observing from the shore, the sailboats on bodies of water such as Nantucket Sound appear to be the picture of carefree tranquility. Little does that observer know of the unceasing alertness required and, yes, even of the tension felt by the skippers guiding their vessels through those shoals.

Cape Cod's harbors are almost as tricky to enter as the sound itself is to navigate, but their beauty and that of the towns they serve make the trip worthwhile.

Chatham, at the Cape's elbow, is a charmer, possibly because it seems less commercial than some of the others in this evermore-crowded vacationland, but possibly also because its Stage Harbor is one of the most interesting—make that hair-raising—to enter.

One comes in from the sound by threading a needle's eye, a channel barely a boat's width wide and so close to the shore that you can reach out and touch the folks fishing or wading there.

Harwich's entrance isn't much wider but inside there are three harbors of

66. *Madaket.*

equal distinction, and just a few miles southwest, if you aren't too deep in the keel, there is one of the Cape's prettiest boat trips up the Bass River, winding through a lush countryside of lovely homes, windmills, and inns.

Picturesque Cotuit and Osterville lie on opposite banks of a horseshoe-shaped harbor with islands in its center. Hyannis and Falmouth are the south shore's commercial centers. Hyannis has the Kennedys (Senator Ted and Ethel and the whole tribe are skilled and avid sailors), and Falmouth has a handsome village green surrounded by the familiar houses of ships' captains.

It is in these Cape villages that one can see in profusion, besides the modified saltbox houses that took the Cape Cod name, examples of the gracefully rambling shingle houses first designed by Henry Hobson Richardson, who, as historians Henry Steele Commager and Samuel Eliot Morison noted, "enjoyed a success greater than any other architect before Frank Lloyd Wright."

Woods Hole, at the Cape's southwestern corner, has several distinctions. It is the home of the world-famed oceanographic institute that bears its name, it is the ferry terminal for the islands, and it overlooks a narrow passage between Buzzards Bay and Nantucket and Vineyard sounds that has terrified skippers since Bartholomew Gosnold first discovered the area almost four hundred years ago.

The rock-rimmed channel takes almost a ninety-degree turn right in the middle, and when the tide is changing and the current is roaring through at near four knots and the huge buoys are almost buried in the turbulence, the challenge is enough to shiver the timbers of the heartiest sailor.

Just off Woods Hole is Hadley Harbor on Naushon Island, a favorite anchorage for cruising boats. At the end of a narrow twisting passage through huge rocks, it is a scene of bucolic bliss. The Forbes family (of whom publisher-adventurer-balloonist-sailor Malcolm Forbes is one) owns the island, and great mansions grace its hilltops like castles on a Scottish moor.

The harbor shore itself, besides the grassy shelf on which horses, cows, and sheep graze, is lined with the support mechanism for an island population—a slip from which the Forbeses' small private ferry runs over to Woods Hole and a boatyard which cares for the fleet of pleasure craft.

The gracious Forbeses not only permit anchorage in their harbor, but they even have set aside one of their small islands on which visiting yachtsmen are invited to stretch their legs.

Hadley's quiet is a welcome refuge on those many days when strong winds whip up the comparatively shallow waters of Buzzards Bay and justify its notoriety as perhaps the Atlantic Coast's roughest sailing ground.

At the other end of the bay, almost-landlocked Marion is another popular

67. *Fishing Fleet.*

68. Nantucket Harbor.

harbor, a peaceful little inlet with no commerce on its shores, only a hospitable yacht club, a couple of small boatyards tucked away in one corner, and big homes with their manicured lawns running to the water.

Marion is a jumping-off place for the run through the Cape Cod Canal. The eight-mile land cut, dug across the narrow isthmus that joined Cape Cod and the mainland, was completed in 1914, ending a century-long feud between rival interests in the ports of New York and Boston. New York wanted the canal in order to shorten by sixty-five miles or more the route to Northern Europe and save sailing vessels the dangerous passage around the shoals of Nantucket and the Cape. Boston felt that giving New York this advantage would reduce its trade with Europe, but with the coming of faster and safer steamships, Boston lost trade to New York anyway and dropped its objections to the canal.

The Massachusetts Bay side of Cape Cod is lined with historic villages:

Sandwich, where a museum displays examples of the famous glass once made there.

69. Standing By.

Pretty little Truro, long popular with artists and writers.

Barnstable, one of the towns that sported a liberty pole around which rebellious colonists gathered. Barnstable's pole disappeared one night, and the principal suspect, an outspoken Tory woman named Abigail Freeman, was tarred and feathered and ridden around town in proper style.

And Wellfleet, a summer resort of a very tidy New England nature; the site where Marconi built his first wireless station which sent his first transatlantic radio message; and once a thriving oyster, cod, and mackerel fishing center. Today it is the shore station for a diving operation recovering an uncounted treasure of gold, silver, and jewels from the pirate ship *Whidah*, which went down just offshore in 1717 reputedly with the loot from fifty-two ships. Despite scores of searches through the years, the wreckage was not located until 1984.

A few miles or more just out of Wellfleet toward Truro there is a high sand plateau. From the top you can see most of the Cape and across to Nantucket Sound. It is a part of the northernmost great stretch of beach on the North

American continent—forty miles of fine sand that reaches from Nauset Heights, just south of Wellfleet, to Provincetown on the tip of the Cape. Henry David Thoreau and scores of lesser writers walked that beach; Edward Hopper and scores of lesser artists painted it. Federal protection, local zoning, a short season, and chilly waters have saved it from becoming another Miami Beach.

Provincetown, on the other hand, has not been saved from its own success. The Pilgrims first landed there, enchanted by the wide harbor "wherein," as one wrote, "a thousand ships may safely ride." But they didn't care much for the area, probably because its sandy soil didn't promise the needed crops, and they pushed on across Massachusetts Bay to the place they called Plymouth.

Provincetown was rediscovered in the 1920s by New York artists and writers, who flocked there in such numbers it was called "Greenwich Village North." Mabel Dodge held court there, Sinclair Lewis tarried there, and Eugene O'Neill's first play, *Bound East for Cardiff,* was produced there.

The Pilgrims and the Bohemians came to Provincetown seeking liberties denied them elsewhere: freedom of religion for the one, freedom of expression for the other.

Both groups left their marks on P-town, as its familiars call it. Families of long New England lineage live in some of the Victorian homes in the side streets, while Commercial Street, the main shopping drag, is a summer carnival that smells of popcorn, saltwater taffy, and cotton candy. It is popular with gays, a seasonal Key West North.

Provincetown today also has a comparatively new and thriving industry—whale watching. Every day during the season sight-seeing boats go out a mere seven miles to the Stellwagen Bank, where large numbers of finback and humpback whales spend the summer. Apparently unaffected by man's proximity, they put on a spectacular show, breaching and sounding within a few hundred feet of the spectator fleet. The tour is now getting so popular, however, that the experts are becoming concerned that the whales might be disturbed by the visitors.

We had an extraordinary experience off the Cape's Atlantic shore a few years ago. *Wyntje* was under power on one of those hazy, hot, windless days without a ripple on the ocean, when suddenly we were surrounded by whales. Appearing above water and then diving again they were impossible to count, but it seemed that there were scores of them as far as the eye could penetrate the haze.

At one point two of them bracketed us and swam alongside not a hundred feet away. I think they were fins. They were longer than our forty-two-foot boat, certainly big enough to unintentionally swamp us.

70. The Old Harbor Light.

They were with us for perhaps half an hour before we left them behind. And then within a few minutes we just as suddenly were surrounded by dolphins, and now it seemed there were hundreds of them. First one pair and then another would come alongside to pay us a visit and play around our bow. As always with these delightful creatures, we regretted the moment they decided to say goodbye.

It is twenty miles, barely a half-day's sail, from Provincetown across to Plymouth, the last stage of the Pilgrims' two-month voyage from England. Whether that sick and weary band really scrambled ashore across what is now called Plymouth Rock is questionable, but unquestioned is that the rock is a tourist mecca. The proof is that people throw coins at it. One of nature's mysteries is why tourists throw coins at any small body of water they can look down upon—fountains, wells, fishponds.

Docked nearby is a life-sized replica of the Pilgrims' *Mayflower*, and it is worth a visit to appreciate the discomfort suffered by those 102 souls crammed on its tiny deck and packed into a common cabin with barely room to stand. No matter what they thought of Provincetown, it is a wonder that once ashore anything could have persuaded them to climb back aboard that floating prison.

Pleasingly colonial Duxbury, two miles across Plymouth Bay, almost certainly was the nation's first suburb. It was founded by some of the Pilgrims who fled the growing "urbanization" of Plymouth. Today, with Scituate and Cohasset, it is one of the chain of harbors favored by Boston yachtsmen.

The American who can sail into Boston Harbor without feeling embraced by history has no feel for history at all. The imagination runs riot as you approach the almost-legendary land of those places of our nation's beginnings, even though you can't really see them from the water anymore. Bunker Hill has been cut down and hidden behind tall buildings; Griffin's Wharf, where the tea was dumped, has disappeared under landfill, as has the dock where John Hancock's ship *Liberty* was seized by the British, touching off some of the earliest rioting.

The *Constitution*, "Old Ironsides," is there though, venerable reminder of our great seafaring heritage, veteran of the 1812 battles that conquered the vaunted British and brought forth a new power on the world's oceans.

Once a year, on July 4, she is towed away from her dock at the old Charlestown Navy Yard and out into the harbor, turned around, and towed back, the exercise to keep her from weathering on one side only. The navy and the people make a big ceremony of it, as they should. The old girl is adorned with flags as she might have been when she sailed out to meet the *Guerrière*, and on her quarterdeck a band plays.

OVERLEAF: *72. Low Tide.*

73. Sankaty Head.

71. Catboat Picnic.

74. *Old Ironsides.*

75. *Dropping the Jib.*

A fleet of horn-tooting spectator boats falls in alongside, and cheering, flag-waving crowds line the shore. At noon there is a salute from the *Constitution*'s antique guns, specially reinforced for the occasion. And across the harbor old Fort Independence's cannons, firing in honor of the holiday, seem to return the salute. It is enough to bring tears of appreciation to an old salt's eyes.

Boston was the first of the northeast ports to renovate its run-down waterfront; today the Constitution and Lewis wharves have been rebuilt, and one can dock for the night almost under the restored market hall that merchant Peter Faneuil gave to the city in 1742.

Intrigued by the grasshopper symbol of the Royal Exchange in London, Faneuil had a large grasshopper placed over the cupola of his building. In the War of 1812, the grasshopper became a password on the waterfront. Anyone who didn't know that it was a symbol of Boston was suspected of being a spy.

A couple of hours' sail out of Boston and the imagination can rest as one picks up a mooring in the crowded harbor of Marblehead. In contrast to Boston's, its waterfront is remarkably untouched by the twentieth century.

Some of the old houses tottering on the winding streets go back to the days when Captain Trevett marched the Marblehead company out to do battle at Bunker Hill. The Lafayette house is so named because a corner had to be cut away to permit the Marquis de Lafayette's carriage to navigate the turn. There are a few bars that evoke the days when "one for the road" frequently turned out to be the Mickey that delivered the unsuspecting patron to a shanghai gang and a long term of servitude at sea.

It is no wonder that this picturesque and lively port has become a favorite of the international yachting fraternity and the principal sailing center of the Boston area. With three major yacht clubs on its shores, it also is one of the most crowded harbors on the East Coast and, when the wind goes around to the northeast, one of the roughest.

Many a night, as a strong nor'easter began to bounce the fleet about, we have pulled our foul-weather gear over our pajamas and gotten underway to make a cold and uncomfortable run the four miles to a haven under the lee at Manchester across the bay.

Around the corner from Marblehead is Salem, which as early as 1664 was referred to by a colonial scribbler as noted for its "rich merchants" and its gabled houses. One with seven gables was made famous by Nathaniel Hawthorne, others for harboring the Salem "witches" or those who condemned them.

Salem's golden years of international trade came immediately after the Revolution when she had 252 vessels in commission, most of them sailing to India

76. Walk to the Light.

77. *Draggers.*

and China in a trade developed by one Elias H. Derby. He successfully defied the monopoly until then held by the East India companies of the Dutch and the English and became America's first millionaire.

Old Derby Street Wharf is still there, and you can put your boat alongside and tie up where Elias's vessels used to be almost two hundred years ago.

Along the twelve miles of rugged coast from Salem to Gloucester, in such communities as Beverly, Prides Crossing, Manchester, and Magnolia, is a mixture of old colonial houses and mansions of this century. Sailing the route up the Cape Ann coast, it is well to steer wide of Norman's Woe Reef. It is there that Henry Wadsworth Longfellow's doomed ship *Hesperus* wrecked.

Gloucester was founded in 1623 as a fishing port and a fishing port it has remained to this day, generations of its men working the rich Georges Bank a hundred miles or more offshore. If it was not already famous, Spencer Tracy, Lionel Barrymore, and Freddie Bartholomew made it so with the 1937 movie *Captains Courageous*, which graphically depicted the hard life of the deep-sea fishermen.

Like New Bedford's, Gloucester's fishing fleet has fallen on hard times in recent years, but through it all the imposing statue of the Gloucester Fisherman stands at the waterfront, his eyes fixed on the ocean that is his life.

Rockport, Gloucester's suburb on the Cape's side, is an artist colony overrun by tourists, most noted for its red fisherman's shack that has been the subject of so many paintings it has become known as Motif Number One.

In 1713, Gloucester gave the world the practical sailboat known as the schooner, but it was at Essex, north of the Cape at Ipswich Bay, that most of the finest Gloucester schooners were built. The yard now is a shipbuilding museum.

The Massachusetts coast runs out just beyond Newburyport, even as that town's fame and prosperity as a major port went out with the clipper ships. In recent years, however, its downtown area has been renovated, and experts on Federalist period architecture say its old captains' houses on High Street are among the finest examples to be found anywhere.

New Hampshire's little window on the ocean is an eighteen-mile stretch of coast most notable for the harbor of Portsmouth, a major shipbuilding center in the last century. Upriver, in the days of wooden ships, ninety sawmills cut the trees from New Hampshire's lush forests into nine million feet of lumber a year to build a good part of America's merchant marine. Today a naval shipyard continues to be active at Portsmouth.

78. *Beacon Street.*

79. *Hulbert Dock.*

80. On the Foredeck.

81. Yard Talk.

Visible from some miles at sea, at the entrance to the Piscataqua River, is the seemingly endless expanse of one of the country's finest old Victorian hotels, Wentworth-by-the-Sea. You can sail right up to its broad grounds and nestle for the night along the shore where the Russian and Japanese diplomats probably strolled between sessions of their peace conference back in 1905. The treaty ending the Russo-Japanese War, the one engineered by Teddy Roosevelt back there at Oyster Bay, was signed at Portsmouth.

From the Wentworth on a clear day you can see the complex of nine small granite islands ten miles out to sea known collectively as the Isles of Shoals. It is an adventure to sail among them, following an otherwise almost unmarked path between the great slabs of grey rock. And, if the timing is right, fields of orange-red poppies crown the bare hills like a May wreath on a bald head.

Almost from the moment of their discovery in 1605, the Isles were a major rendezvous for fishermen from all over Europe. An early historian recorded:

> *Fishing vessels came hither . . . Doggers and Pinckies of the English, clumsy Busses of Holland, light Fly-boats of Flanders, the Biskiner and Portingal and many other odd high-peaked vessels were attracted thither summer after summer.*

Governor John Winthrop noted that in 1634 the Isles settlement's assessed property was equal to that of New Plymouth, and as many as seventeen fishing vessels arrived from Europe in the single month of March.

The islands' serious modern development came in 1848, when one Thomas Laighton established a resort there and became keeper of the lighthouse.

Despite, or maybe because of, the isolation and even bleakness of the place, the resort was something of a success, and by the time Laighton's daughter, Celia Thaxter, was making her mark as a poet toward the end of the century, it was the summer rendezvous of musicians, painters, and writers, Oliver Wendell Holmes and John Greenleaf Whittier among them.

The Thaxter home was on Appledore Island, now the site of a marine research laboratory. The successor to Laighton's resort, a large white frame structure on smaller Star Island, is now a church-run conference center.

Maine begins on the banks of the Piscataqua at Kittery, where in 1777 the first warship commissioned by the fledgling U.S. Navy was launched. Under the audacious command of John Paul Jones, the *Ranger* a year later was sailing in and out of British ports, torching the ships it found and terrorizing the locals.

82. Picnic at Chappaquiddick.

83. The Naushon.

From Kittery to Portland the Maine coast is marked by a trio of keyhole harbors, York, Kennebunkport, and Cape Porpoise, each with its own distinction for the sailing man.

Built-up York is tricky to enter—a sharp right turn and a couple of rocks marking a narrow channel. At artsy Kennebunkport it is worth waiting for high tide to get over the shallow entrance. Picturesque Cape Porpoise has so many lobster traps at its entrance it almost defies entering at all.

Cape Porpoise was the first Maine port into which I sailed uncounted years ago, and I learned two unforgettable lessons that day: First, running over a lobster pot can ruin your whole day, and second, going overboard to cut it loose from your propeller is an exercise only a masochist could enjoy. No warning is strong enough to indicate how cold Maine waters really can be in June.

Just before turning Cape Elizabeth for Portland, one can sail up to the resort community of Prouts Neck for a quick visit to the modest house where Winslow Homer painted many of his famous seascapes.

Portland's waterfront, a few years ago a disaster area, has been faithfully restored as part of the city's vigorous redevelopment program. The old cobbled streets at the docks now lead up to several blocks of ancient mercantile buildings housing coffee shops, restaurants, and boutiques.

There are those who will tell you that as you sail out of Portland you finally have reached the "real Maine." Others will claim that the "real Maine" begins somewhere farther east. This is part of a Mainiacal one-upmanship practised by cruising sailors who find that part of the joy in voyaging is going somewhere others have not.

The only way to beat their game is to sail off the Maine chart into Canada, but the truth is that the sailor's Maine, the "real Maine," is right there out of Portland Harbor where Casco Bay begins.

Maine is a sailing paradise, and the roughly 240 square miles of Casco Bay, dotted with its 365 islands, is a sampler of its joys. The cool air is so clean that a city dweller's lungs want to burst with the marvel of it; the water is so clear you can see the lobsters scurry over the bottom; the winds rise on most days to take you on silent wings of canvas to new delights.

A daylong voyage from Portland through the labyrinth of Casco's islands brings us to one of my favorite anchorages, and for a first night it holds the

Rye Bluffs - New Hampshire

promise of so many more just like it to come. It lies off the bay down a narrow corridor between the rocks, with the dark green spruce and cedar forming overhead a canopy that almost shuts out the summer's bright sun.

Inside, the passage opens into a small lagoon, the corridor is swallowed by the trees, and we seem to be alone on a lake suspended in space and time. The splash of the anchor is an intrusion. A loon, watching from the near shore, takes its leave with a crazy cry.

The air is warmer here, away from the ocean winds, and a test of the water even invites a swim—brief, but a swim. From the cockpit, the evening libation in hand, we watch the fish ripple the water as they pursue their evening meal.

A pair of ducks appear from nowhere, and we dive below for the bread we've saved for this occasion. Soon our apparently grateful ducks are joined by a half-dozen sea gulls that, with unexpectedly good manners, hang back and wait for second table.

The smell of our dinner on the galley stove doesn't fight but rather complements the sweet sunset fragrance of the damp forest, and it foretells an evening around the table with good talk and good wine and the overhead kerosene lamp warming us with its soft glow.

Abed, under a blanket or two, we're sent to sleep by a gentle wind just strong enough to ripple the water against our hull and speed a whisper through the trees.

We'd have to get up mighty early to enjoy a morning as peaceful as the night, for dawn brings the lobstermen and their chugging engines and the radios they play at maximum volume so they can hear them over those engines.

84. *White Dory.*

85. Winter Comes.

The lobstermen and their efficient little craft are everywhere in Maine waters, and as we sail on down east and the day grows longer, we'll be hailing one of them to buy some of their fresh catch, and the evening will find us partaking of one of the seas' greatest gifts to mankind.

Not everybody, it turns out, likes lobsters. They are the only thing about Maine, as nearly as I can make out, that our dear friend and sailing buddy, television's Gary Moore, doesn't like. He refuses to eat them. He calls them "seagoing cockroaches."

There will be other anchorages similar to our first and some others of equal charm but different character. There are the bigger towns (although none in Maine are very large) such as Boothbay Harbor, Camden, and Bar Harbor with their busy, crowded waterfronts and their charms almost buried under summer tourists. Camden is home port for the windjammers that take the venturesome for one-week cruises and bring to Maine's waters a touch of days past.

Northeast Harbor demands a stop, gateway as it is to Mount Desert Island and Frenchman Bay and, with its superbly run municipal marina, in its own right a worthy destination.

Around the corner is the deep fjord known as Somes Sound, and at its head is one of Maine's prettiest harbors. A narrow keyhole is its entry. Spectacular homes cantilevered over the rocks adorn one shore, and Mount Desert's oldest town, Somesville, sits delicately on the other.

Somes Sound Harbor is an example of the Maine harbors of limited facilities but unique attractions. I'm thinking particularly of Christmas Cove, up the Damariscotta River a short distance above Linekin Neck, where Mike Mitchell and his family, refugees from Madison Avenue, run a restaurant that has become a mandatory stop for cruising yachtsmen. Christmas Cove was given its lovely name by the peripatetic Captain John Smith who, guess what, spent Christmas Day there in 1614.

Special, too, is Castine up in the northeast corner of Penobscot Bay. It nestles on the side of the hill looking down on its natural harbor, its main street climbing past the one-junction business section to the brow of the hill and the neat, green campus of the Maine Maritime Academy. The academy's big training vessel, a troop transport ship used in the Korean War, rests much of the year next to the town dock.

It sits not far from where the young American navy suffered one of its worst defeats of the Revolution, an unsuccessful attempt in 1779 to drive the British from Castine.

Castine was heavily loyalist in the Revolutionary War, and when its residents learned that the boundaries of the new nation included them they took down their houses, board by board, loaded them on scows, and towed them across the new boundary, the St. Croix River, to St. Andrews on the "safe" side of Passamaquoddy Bay. Their descendants are there today.

Very special are the little harbors with one- or two-store villages (if, indeed, there are any stores at all) where the summer people moor their boats alongside the working lobstermen. Sorrento is one we are fond of, where there is nothing ashore but comfortable homes, hospitable friends, and a long walk to the highway, and where one night we lay on the deck until dawn watching the heavens fill with an incredible display of the aurora borealis.

Another anchorage is a favorite of ours not only for its beauty but more particularly for the friends there. Russell Wiggins and his wife, Mabel, are natives of Minnesota but have become as much a part of Maine as if their ancestors had settled there a century or two ago.

Russell bought the Ellsworth *American* in 1966 when he retired as managing editor of the *Washington Post*. With his meticulous editing, high reportorial standards, and his own editorials and particularly splendid verse on everything from man's follies to the beauty of a Maine winter, he has turned it into perhaps the best weekly newspaper in the country.

Their lovely, sprawling old farm home on the banks of the Benjamin River at Brooklin has become a mecca for their hundreds of friends from across the country—partly because of Mabel's infectious good humor, but also to no small degree because of her irresistible three-bean salad and blueberry pies.

Russell still sails his beloved Friendship sloop. Built in 1904, it is believed to be the second oldest of this venerable Maine boat in existence. He has sailed it, alone much of the time, up and down the Maine coast pursuing his insatiable quest for local lore.

His unflagging high spirits usually break through the Yankee reserve of his neighbors, but not always. He tells of the day he was sailing up to an abandoned stone pier in a little-used harbor. His approach was watched silently by an oldtimer standing on the dock looking for all the world like the model of those kitsch wooden figures you can buy at any New England souvenir stand—the

86. Behind the Shed.

87. *Boiling Surf.*

88. *Christmas Cove.*

89. Morning Caller.

Maine (or Gloucester or New Bedford or Nantucket) fisherman with his grey beard and his yellow hat and coat and boots. Suddenly Russ fetched up hard on a rock barely fifty feet from the dock.

"I've gone aground," Russ yelled to the old-timer.

Removing the pipe from his mouth, the old-timer answered, "Thought ya would."

Around the corner from the Benjamin River, up Eggemoggin Reach, one can find the ruins of one of the ice factories that in the last century shipped Maine ice around the world. Cut in huge pieces from freshwater ponds in the hills above the reach, the ice was lowered by railway to a stone dock below where large sailing ships waited for the valuable cargo. Packed in sawdust in the hold and naturally cooled by the ocean waters outside, enough survived the long trip to provide luxurious Maine ice even for the British colonists in India.

Ice was a big Maine export in the days before electric refrigeration, taking its place just slightly behind timber, shipbuilding, and fishing as a major industry.

Back up the treelined road along the coast behind the Wigginses' house is an unprepossessing clapboard church with a modest steeple where, if the visiting yachtsman should be fortunate enough, an exciting evening of Americana may be experienced.

At irregular intervals and apparently inspired just by the whim of a member, an evening sing is organized. A simple hand-lettered cardboard sign posted on the

90. Near Thomaston.

fence in front announces the event, and on the evening appointed, the church fills early. The leader calls out the number of the first tune, and the assembled audience seems to know the number and the words so well that its members scarcely need the hymnals in front of them. And after the first selection, they call out the number they would like to do next, and it is done.

It strikes one, in this environment where so many of the participants earn their living from the sea and have seen so many kin go down to it never to return, how many of our American and British hymns have a nautical flavor.

At Lash's yard in Friendship, you can have one of the handsome little sloops like Russ's built on order. Friendship is a pretty village perched above a working lobster harbor, and Lash's Boatyard sits on a curve of the road just outside of town.

A visit there is something of a disappointment, or perhaps, in the unpretentious milieu of Maine, it should be called a pleasant surprise. Totally unmarked by a sign of any kind, it is a big, weathered shed that threatens to slide down its own railway across the rocks to the water below.

On our last visit there we found the doors wide open but not a soul inside. There was an old powerboat apparently in for repairs. Tools were lying about, half-covered with sawdust. Most of them looked as if they had come from an antique exhibit at a marine museum, but we knew they were the instruments of artists.

91. Puffins.

In the town of Friendship there is a sign noting the mileage to some other Maine communities. It says: "Freedom 45; Liberty 33; Harmony 96; Unity 52; Union 20; Hope 27. Friendship is here."

There are Maine historians who take some umbrage over the attention given Plymouth as the first settlement on the American shore. Though acknowledging that the intended permanence of the Plymouth Colony bestows its uniqueness, they point out that many fishing camps were established by the British, Portuguese, Dutch, and others in Maine some years before Plymouth was founded, and many of these had the character of permanent villages.

In fact, they note the camps were so well known that in their first terribly hard winter, the Plymouth colonists sent a boat up to Maine to buy fish to tide them over.

Most of those early fishing camps were on the islands that pepper the waters off the Maine coast—forbidding and mostly barren rocks of various sizes; some, those without natural harbors, uninhabited; others, where there is some shelter into which to bring a boat, with a half-dozen or a dozen hardy families who year-round eke a living from the sea and send their children by boat across miles of open sea for schooling.

The larger islands, such as Monhegan, Isleboro, North Haven, and Vinalhaven, now host large communities of summer residents. Monhegan has been popular with several generations of noted artists. Rockwell Kent's old home is now that of Jamie Wyeth. Ray is not the only artist to have been intrigued by the starkness of Manana Island as seen from Monhegan.

Ray's favorite, and one of mine, is Ragged Island—barely a mile long, one of the smaller outcroppings of rock that can sustain life. Its tiny harbor has an entrance that, if not in configuration at least in difficulty of entry, is typical of the islands. It is barely a boat length wide, and hidden rocks guard the shores. When the wind is from the north and the sea is making up it is a dangerous entry, and even under ideal conditions on a lovely, fog-free summer day, the ocean surge threatens to lift the unwary yachtsman out of control onto those feared rocks.

Once inside, the harbor is cozy but crowded with the dozen or so lobster boats that make this home.

Like some giant's backyard fishpond, the almost-circular harbor is lined with granite boulders. The only access to shore, unless one wants to chance rowing his dinghy up on those rocks, is via the wooden dock that reaches out into the harbor. As with all of the piers in this part of the world where the tides run fifteen feet or more, at low tide its spindly structure seems to defy gravity. The climb from the boat below up its perpendicular wooden ladder is not for the fainthearted.

It seemed almost too crowded for *Wyntje*'s forty-two feet when first we sailed into Ragged Island Harbor; maneuvering was tricky and uncomfortable in the little basin and made particularly difficult by the long mooring lines that the lobstermen had stretched across the harbor.

A young lobsterman unloading his boat of the day's catch saw our dilemma and, waving to one of the moorings ahead of him, shouted, "Pick it up. He's gone to Rockland. Won't be back tonight."

We gratefully accepted the offer and were lying comfortably to the line when the tide began to fall, and a huge rock began creeping into view under our stern. The tidal fall stopped as we had but inches between us and impalement.

So precipitous are some of the harbor's rock ledges that the depth sounder in the center of the boat, as in our case, might show plenty of water while there is none off either end.

From the dock appears one of those visual vignettes that constantly delight the visitor to Maine. With the tide running out, the long mats of seaweed flow back and forth into beautiful patterns of green between the rocks, as if some celestial surrealist were playing at his palette.

Past the modest houses of the lobstermen nestled around the harbor, one climbs up over the hill to see stretched below the whole breadth of the Atlantic, the waves it generates off Portugal finally fetching up on Ragged's rocks with a crunching assault that appears to threaten to push the tiny island off its granite base.

Part of Ragged Island's charm is in the derivation of its name. Some Maine historians such as Charles B. McLane assume that it can be traced back to the Abnaki Indian name for "island rocks," *raggertask*. From this came the British seaman's natural translation to "ragged ass."

That gave way to the more colloquial "ragged arse" and, indeed, as Ragged Arse it was shown on the pre-Revolutionary charts. It is still called that by lobstermen of the area, although mapmakers of Puritan bent in the early days of the Republic charted it as simply Ragged Island. That name sticks, but officially it has been Criehaven, after a founder, since its 1896 incorporation.

The chain of larger islands forms a virtual gold coast of wealthy summer homeowners. Rockefellers, Astors, Morgans, Vanderbilts, and scores of others of almost equal fame populate the area in July and August. They all seem to play a game of one-upmanship as to who has been coming to Maine the longest, although most of them count their years there in generations. And their traditions run deep.

In the 1880s, the rich vacationers on North Haven commissioned a local shipwright named J. O. Brown to build them a fifteen-foot day sailer they would

92. Loon.

93. Homage to Homer.

94. Gibby Alley . . . Lobsterman.

call the North Haven dinghy. Now, more than a century later, the North Haven dinghy continues to be raced in the Penobscot Bay waters off North Haven, probably by grandchildren and great-grandchildren of the original owners. And three generations of descendants of J. O. Brown are building boats there today.

North Haven's twin island of Vinalhaven (they are separated only by the busy channel known as Fox Island Thoroughfare) has its share of well-to-do summer people, but I like to think its greatest fame is that the Carvers, who gave their name to Carvers Harbor, were probably the world's biggest horsenet manufacturers. Horsenets kept flies off horses, a matter which bothered a considerable population of horses at one time.

According to Bill Caldwell, Portland *Press Herald* columnist and author of innumerable fascinating books on Maine lore, more than a thousand persons worked for the Carvers making horsenets not only on Vinalhaven but at Port Clyde and on Deer Isle. Of course, Henry Ford put a stop to all that.

The Maine islands were the subject of great real estate speculations as early as Revolutionary times, and Caldwell tells the tale of the most fascinating of all the speculators.

Colonel James Swan is a much-overlooked figure of our early history. He was a Revolutionary War hero, an abolitionist a half-century before his time, and a dreamer who envisioned an empire of prosperous islands of which one that he modestly named "Swan's" would be the centerpiece.

His dream collapsed, and he fled to Paris to escape his debts. There he raised money for the young American Republic but once again overspent, this time ending up in debtors' prison. For twenty-two years he lived, rather than languished, in prison. Using funds sent him by his wife in America, he sponsored lavish parties for his French friends outside the prison. Of course, he himself could not attend. He asked only that an empty chair be held for him at the head of the table and that a toast be drunk to him.

Out to sea a way from Ragged Island is an even smaller island, so small, in fact, that it is only called a rock—Matinicus Rock. There are no people on it, but thousands of tourists come to visit its inhabitants each summer. They are the Disneyesque little birds known as puffins, colorful Harlequins in their bold black-and-white plumage with white face and breast, bright orange webbed feet, red-ringed eyes, and beaks with a blue base, tipped in orange.

They come to Matinicus to breed for a few weeks each year. They are scarce, and landing on the island, even if its sharp cliff would permit, is discouraged. But this is hardly necessary anyway. On a calm day they swim surprisingly close to your boat. When they catch a fish you get a good view of them,

95. Rolling In.

97. The Sailmaker.

96. Poppies.

98. Lash's Boatyard.

99. Lobsterman's Cove.

their struggling meal clasped in their beaks, making a quick reconnaissance flight along the cliffside before suddenly disappearing into the particular crevice where they nest.

Speaking of birds, fall is a wonderful time to sail almost anywhere but is particularly rewarding in Maine. Although its waters are never really crowded, in fall almost the last summer sailor has gone. One can sail all day without seeing another boat, and the anchorages are delightfully empty.

But a special bonus is the geese and ducks rafting up, organizing, getting their orders, it seems, for the migration south. It fills a human with envy to know that they will make their trip without listening to an interminable concert of canned music while waiting "for the next available reservation clerk."

Every winter as we sail south and watch in admiration as the great flights of geese pass overhead in the V formation, a veteran of our crew, Fred Celce, asks the newcomer, "Do you know why one side of the V is longer than the other?"

"No, why?" asks the innocent freshman.

"More ducks."

The islands of Maine are frequently in such clusters that they form an intriguing mystic maze that would draw the admiration of a puzzle maker or a British gardener.

Once we sailed from Martha's Vineyard directly to Maine, making our landfall as planned at the southwestern corner of Penobscot Bay for a rendezvous with Mike Forrestal on his *Belle*. Mike has been sailing those waters all his life and knows them intimately. At the appointed hour, he radioed for our position. I gave it to him and remarked that his radio transmission was coming in good and strong.

"It ought to be," he replied. "I'm about five hundred yards from you, just on the other side of the island you are now passing to port."

The British navy and American privateers played hide-and-seek here, and down through history to this very day smugglers have island-hopped their illicit goods past harried government agents.

It was in the knot of little islands off Stonington that Charles and Anne Lindbergh found seclusion for their honeymoon. They slipped away from the summer estate of her father, Dwight Morrow, on North Haven and sailed to a lovely cove on McGlathery Island as the newshawks searched frantically for them.

Navigation among the islands is tricky enough on clear days, but it can be harrowing on those frequent days of fog. It may come in on cat feet as Carl Sandburg insisted, but it has the viciousness of a mother tiger at bay.

100. The Privy.

101. *Raspberries.*

A Maine fog can come up in minutes with smothering density. The bow of your boat and the top of your mast disappear, and you are cast adrift in an impenetrable sea of white.

However, the old-time sailors in Maine, and particularly the lobstermen, go plunging about in the fog with unearthly ability to find their way. I asked a lobsterman how in the world he did it.

"How do you know where the rocks are?" I asked.

"Don't," he answered. "I know where they ain't."

A fellow yachtsman tells of asking the same question of a lobsterman. His answer was somewhat different.

"Why," he bragged, "I know every rock in Muscle Ridge Channel." With that the lobster boat bounced off a submerged rock.

"There's one now," continued the lobsterman, without missing a beat.

That might have been Wiggins Rock, which Russ Wiggins insists was not named for him. If you are a sailor, it is not a good thing to have a rock named after you.

Of course the modern miracles of navigation, radar, and loran have taken much of the danger out of the fog, but care still is needed. The radar set on *Wyntje* is below in a conveniently darkened navigation room, and the radar operator, usually me, communicates to the helmsman in the cockpit by radio.

102. *Seal Cove.*

103. Foul-Weather Gear.

My wife and one of my favorite companions, Bill Harbach, have a lot to live down for their treatment of their captain on one foggy day as we were sailing around Mount Desert. I was below calling up instructions:

"All right, steer 265 and you have a buoy about one-quarter mile ahead." A pause. "Okay, do you see the buoy?"

"Yep," Bill would answer. "Right on it. What next?"

"Steer 287—a black buoy another quarter of a mile."

This went on for a half-hour or so when, at an open stretch of water, I chose to get a breath of fresh air above decks. I emerged into bright sunlight!

"When did the fog clear?" I asked in amazement.

"Oh," Bill innocently replied, "about twenty minutes ago."

A summer visitor at Bass Harbor took a small boat out on an average Maine day, only to be helplessly lost in the fog. He came ashore on Great Gott Island and called for help, "Is there anyone here? Is there anyone here?"

Mrs. Gott heard his cry at her house on the hill and came down through the fog to the rocks below to find her unexpected visitor standing beside his boat.

"May I introduce myself?" he said. "I'm Admiral Byrd."

So famous was he then, he did not need to identify himself as the great explorer who had found his way through the uncharted wilderness of Antarctica but had lost his way in a Maine fog.

If the fog is thick elsewhere, it seems to be twice as thick and at least twice as frequent east of Schoodic.

"East of Schoodic" is familiar Maine nomenclature. The peninsula that juts out as the eastern boundary of Frenchman Bay is named Schoodic after an early Indian tribe. It divides the Maine coast into two parts as distinctively, for the sailor at least, as the Rockies divide the continent.

East of Schoodic the tides, like the fog, seem to run stronger, the waves are higher, the rockbound coast is even rockier, and the harbors of refuge are fewer and harder of entry. And inland the country is not so forested, not so green.

For all these reasons this area hasn't known the growth of summer colonies with anything like the profusion found west of Schoodic. The natives, mostly fishermen, are as rugged a race as you'll find in North America. Although they are fiercely independent, they are quick to extend a helping hand to the sailor in need, as Ray found when he nearly went on the rocks at Moose Peak Light in a dense fog, and lobsterman David Look came upon him and led him to safety.

The first major port sailing eastward from Schoodic is Jonesport, famous for its lobster boats that are higher in the bow and narrower of beam than boats built elsewhere.

104. Meadow by the Church.

106. Rebuilding at Jonesport.

105. Winter's Wood.

107. Island Overlook.

108. Root Cellar.

The Jonesport lobstermen equip them with the biggest automobile engines they can find, and they have an extraordinary turn of speed. One coming at you, plunging through the whitecaps with a curtain of spray from that formidable bow, and you think you are being run down by a destroyer.

Just beyond Jonesport is Roque Island, something of a geographical anomaly. This almost-perfect crescent forms a well-protected bay, which can be a welcome haven in this area. But the salient feature is the beach.

On Maine's rocky coast, sand beaches are pocket-sized. They can be measured in feet, if not in inches. But Roque's beach is wide and the sand is soft, and it even seems that the water is warmer than elsewhere—that is, survivable by the hardy.

The harbors east of Roque are not without some charm and definitely are prominent in our history.

Our first naval engagement almost certainly came at Machias. When the news of Lexington arrived in the busy little town, its four hundred or so souls erected a liberty pole and were promptly ordered to take it down by Captain Moore of HMS *Margaretta*, which happened to be in port.

109. Breaking Through.

The incensed people of Machias chased Moore back to his vessel and jeered his departure, working themselves up into such a lather of patriotic fervor that forty of them, a few with muskets but most with pitchforks, piled aboard the sloop *Unity* lying at the wharf and set sail in pursuit under the command of fiery patriot Jeremiah O'Brien.

They were still within sight of shore when the faster *Unity* overtook the *Margaretta* and, despite the Britisher's fourteen swivel guns, let loose a broadside of musket fire. A lucky shot hit the *Margaretta*'s helmsman, the schooner broached, O'Brien ran his bowsprit through the Britisher's sail, and with the boats thus locked together, the Americans swarmed aboard brandishing their pitchforks.

The experienced British sailors may have faced muskets and bayonets but not pitchforks. They panicked and surrendered the ship—a first for Machias and for a brand new nation.

By the way, many of the nation's blueberries come from the barrens of Washington County behind Machias, the county seat.

Machias is more famous recently for a bitter battle waged over the dreams of some to establish in its deep water a port for supertankers. Environmentalists successfully fought the plan, not the least of their concern being the fear of catastrophic spills that could endanger the precious bird sanctuary off Machias.

Along with Matinicus Rock, Machias's bird sanctuary has a thriving puffin population as well as a handsome gathering of those crossword-puzzle birds, auks, known more familiarly as razorbills. Standing upright and decked out in white shirt and black suits, they look amazingly like child-birds playing at being penguins.

Modern science has encroached on Cutler, thirteen miles on eastward. The hills above that lovely inlet are now marked by twenty-six huge towers spotted over a 2,800-acre site—the most powerful radio sending station in the world and the navy's vital link with its submarines prowling the ocean deeps. What a far cry from the lighthouses that beamed their messages barely to the horizon!

Fifteen miles farther along the United States comes to an end, not with the whispering gentleness of Key West at the other end of the eastern frontier but with the deafening crash of waves beating against the rocks below the candy-striped lighthouse at West Quoddy Head, the nation's easternmost point.

The nearest town is Lubec, once a prosperous sardine-canning center. It is the gateway to Campobello, the Canadian island where Franklin D. Roosevelt summered and where he contracted the polio that crippled him.

In his youth he was an avid sailor. Undoubtedly from a young lifetime of fighting the fierce tides that run through Cobscook Bay, he conjured up the dream that was to lead to one of his most vigorous congressional battles, one he was doomed to lose. That was his grandiose scheme to dam the Cobscook at Passamaquoddy and harness the eighteen-foot tides. He contended enough electricity could be generated to power most of the East Coast.

Although the rising sun first touches the United States at the peak of Maine's over-five-thousand-foot-high Mount Katahdin, many, perhaps most, of the tourists who visit the Eastport, Lubec, and Quoddy Head region arrange to get up before dawn at least once in order to share its distinction of being the first populated area in the United States bathed in the new day's light.

"You people who live here must sort of take a pride in that," I suggested to an older resident watching with me as the tide surged around the bridge pilings at Lubec.

"Well," he said, "tell the truth, never thought much about it."

Catalogue

Paintings are listed consecutively as they appear in the book. Sizes shown are in inches, with vertical measurement first. Unless otherwise indicated, the paintings and drawings are owned by Ray Ellis.

1. (Title Page) *Working the Ledges*. Penobscot Bay, Maine. Watercolor. 1985. 21½ × 29. Private Collection.

2. (Copyright Page) *Alone*. Off Hyannis Port, Massachusetts. Oil. 1983. 20 × 37. Private Collection.

3. *Sutton Place in Winter*. New York, New York. Watercolor. 1982. 14 × 18. Collection of the Heckscher Museum, Huntington, New York. Gift of Mr. Richard Ellis.

4. *Brant Point Beach*. Nantucket, Massachusetts. Watercolor. 1985. 21½ × 33½. Collection of Mr. and Mrs. John Akers.

5. *Through the Inlet*. Atlantic City, New Jersey. Watercolor. 1985. 26 × 39.

6. *Yellow Umbrella*. New Jersey. Oil. 1984. 8½ × 11½. Collection of Mr. and Mrs. George L. Shinn.

7. *Cape May Victorian*. Cape May, New Jersey. Watercolor. 1971. 9½ × 11¾.

8. *Suppertime*. Cape May, New Jersey. Watercolor. 1984. 25 × 33½. Collection of Mr. and Mrs. Edward B. McLaughlin.

9. *Beach at Bay Head*. Bay Head, New Jersey. Watercolor. 1985. 13 × 14. Collection of Mr. and Mrs. John D. Bowe.

10. *Day at the Beach*. New Jersey. Oil. 1984. 9 × 12.

11. *On the Inlet*. New Jersey. Watercolor. 1970. 21 × 29.

12. *Coffee Break*. New Jersey. Oil. 1981. 11 × 14.

13. *Fishing Dock*. Cold Spring Harbor, New Jersey. Watercolor. 1972. 7½ × 11½.

14. *Path to the Point*. Cape May, New Jersey. Watercolor. 1984. 15 × 20.

15. *South Street Seaport*. New York, New York. Watercolor. 1984. 11 × 10.

16. *Battery Ferry*. New York, New York. Watercolor. 1985. 14½ × 24.

17. *Miss Liberty*. New York, New York. Watercolor. 1986. 19 × 29. Collection of Swanke Hayden Connell Architects. Architects for the restoration of the Statue of Liberty.

18. *Hell Gate*. New York, New York. Watercolor. 1984. 9½ × 13½.

19. *New York Harbor*. New York, New York. Oil. 1984. 18 × 24. Collection of Mr. and Mrs. Dennis Jackson.

20. *East Side in Rain*. New York, New York. Watercolor. 1981. 21 × 29. Collection of Wayne C. Spear.

21. *Antique Shop*. Long Island, New York. Watercolor. 1981. 16½ × 21¾. Collection of James N. Richardson, Jr.

22. *Little Harbor*. Long Island, New York. Watercolor. 1984. 10 × 12.

23. *Old Water Tower*. Cold Spring Harbor, Long Island, New York. Watercolor. 1985. 12 × 8.

24. *Fall at Cold Spring*. Cold Spring Harbor, Long Island, New York. Oil. 1985. 9 × 13. Private Collection.

25. *The Bell*. Larchmont, New York. Watercolor. 1985. 25 × 21.

26. *Napping*. Sag Harbor, Long Island, New York. Watercolor. 1984. 15½ × 24. Collection of the Artist.

27. *Winter . . . Lloyd Neck*. Huntington, Long Island, New York. Watercolor. 1985. 13 × 27½.

28. *Mist at Eatons Neck*. Long Island, New York. Watercolor. 1984. 10 × 12.

29. *The Boathouse*. Amityville, Long Island, New York. Watercolor. 1984. 24 × 38½. Collection of Johnson & Higgins.

30. *Mussel Pickers*. Cold Spring Harbor, Long Island, New York. Watercolor. 1984. 22 × 29½. Private Collection.

31. *Walking the Flats*. Oyster Bay, Long Island, New York. Watercolor. 1982. 13 × 22.

32. *Seawanhaka Yacht Club*. Long Island, New York. Watercolor. 1985. 15½ × 24½. Private Collection.

33. *First Snow*. Northport, Long Island, New York. Watercolor. 1985. 18½ × 24. Collection of Mr. and Mrs. John H. Nichols, Jr.

34. *Harbor Roses*. Long Island, New York. Watercolor. 1981. 18½ × 25. Private Collection.

35. *Montauk Light*. Montauk, Long Island, New York. Watercolor. 1984. 17½ × 21½.

36. *Beach Walker*. Shelter Island, Long Island, New York. Watercolor. 1984. 24 × 38½. Collection of Mr. and Mrs. Alan Cassidy.

37. *Sunlit Beach*. Long Island, New York.
Oil. 1984. 8 × 10.
Private Collection.

38. *Sag Harbor Yacht Club*. Long Island, New York.
Watercolor. 1984. 14½ × 22.

39. *Montauk Dunes*. Montauk, Long Island, New York.
Oil. 1984. 19½ × 29½.
Private Collection.

40. *Coming Ashore*. Essex, Connecticut.
Watercolor. 1985. 16 × 21.

41. *Beached Schooner*. Darien, Connecticut.
Watercolor. 1985. 18½ × 25.

42. *The Harbor Light*. Mystic, Connecticut.
Watercolor. 1985. 9 × 25.

43. *Harbor Road*. Stratford, Connecticut.
Watercolor. 1985. 8 × 15.

44. *Painting the Hull*. Galilee, Rhode Island.
Watercolor. 1985. 13 × 9.

45. *Block Island Ruins*. Block Island, Rhode Island.
Watercolor. 1973. 22 × 37.
Collection of L. L. Harrison.

46. *North Point Light*. Block Island, Rhode Island.
Watercolor. 1971. 20 × 33½.
Collection of Allied-Signal Inc.

47. *Ida Lewis Yacht Club*. Newport, Rhode Island.
Watercolor. 1985. 12 × 24.

48. *The Black Pearl*. Newport, Rhode Island.
Oil. 1985. 20 × 24.

49. *In From the Fog*. Off Newport, Rhode Island.
Watercolor. 1984. 23 × 39.
Collection of Mr. and Mrs. John A. Long.

50. *Fishing the Surf*. Newport, Rhode Island.
Watercolor. 1985. 16½ × 24.

51. *Beached Dinghies*. Cuttyhunk Island, Massachusetts.
Watercolor. 1984. 21¾ × 24¼.
Collection of Mr. and Mrs. Gene Simpson.

52. *Flower Cart*. Nantucket, Massachusetts.
Watercolor. 1985. 17 × 25.

53. *Morning Haze*. Martha's Vineyard, Massachusetts.
Oil. 1982. 36 × 48.
Private Collection.

54. *Heading Out*. Martha's Vineyard, Massachusetts.
Watercolor. 1984. 34½ × 24.

55. *Gathering Butterfly Weed*. Martha's Vineyard, Massachusetts. Oil. 1985. 12 × 16.
Collection of Alan L. Miller.

56. *Kingdom by the Sea*. Cape Cod, Massachusetts.
Watercolor. 1983. 12 × 16.
Collection of Claudia Paschal.

57. *Underweigh at Dawn*. Martha's Vineyard, Massachusetts.
Watercolor. 1983. 22¾ × 37.
Private Collection.

58. *The Potting Shed*. Martha's Vineyard, Massachusetts.
Oil. 1985. 25¾ × 37½.
Collection of Marjorie Fiedler.

59. *Edgartown Departure*. Martha's Vineyard, Massachusetts.
Watercolor. 1984. 19½ × 28½.

60. *After Colors*. Martha's Vineyard, Massachusetts.
Oil. 1985. 40 × 50.
Collection of Johnson & Higgins.

61. *Island Morning*. Vineyard Sound, Massachusetts.
Oil. 1984. 36 × 48.
Collection of Mr. and Mrs. Louis Cabot.

62. *Park Street Church*. Boston, Massachusetts.
Watercolor. 1985. 10 × 7.

63. *The Moors*. Tuckernuck Island, Massachusetts.
Oil. 1984. 9½ × 22.

64. *Siasconset Lane*. Nantucket, Massachusetts.
Watercolor. 1984. 9 × 12.
Collection of David T. Sowden.

65. *Nantucket Basket*. Nantucket, Massachusetts.
Watercolor. 1985. 10 × 15.

66. *Madaket*. Nantucket, Massachusetts.
Oil. 1985. 9 × 12.

67. *Fishing Fleet*. Provincetown, Massachusetts.
Oil. 1985. 20 × 24.

68. *Nantucket Harbor*. Nantucket, Massachusetts.
Watercolor. 1985. 15 × 21.
Collection of Mr. and Mrs. Elliott Gumaer, Jr.

69. *Standing By*. Cape Cod, Massachusetts.
Watercolor. 1983. 6½ × 10½.

70. *The Old Harbor Light*. Newburyport, Massachusetts.
Oil. 1985. 9 × 12.

71. *Catboat Picnic*. Martha's Vineyard, Massachusetts.
Oil. 1986. 20 × 30.

72. *Low Tide*. Duxbury, Massachusetts.
Watercolor. 1985. 16 × 29.

73. *Sankaty Head*. Nantucket, Massachusetts.
Oil. 1984. 20 × 25.

74. *Old Ironsides*. Boston, Massachusetts.
Watercolor. 1984. 7 × 10½.

75. *Dropping the Jib*. Martha's Vineyard, Massachusetts.
Oil. 1982. 24 × 36.
Private Collection.

76. *Walk to the Light*. Martha's Vineyard, Massachusetts.
Oil. 1984. 36 × 36.
Collection of Mr. and Mrs. Louis Cabot.

77. *Draggers*. Gloucester, Massachusetts.
Oil. 1984. 8 × 10.

78. *Beacon Street*. Boston, Massachusetts.
Watercolor. 1984. 15 × 23.

79. *Hulbert Dock*. Nantucket, Massachusetts.
Watercolor. 1985. 22 × 33¼.

80. *On the Foredeck*. Nantucket Sound, Massachusetts.
Watercolor. 1985. 15½ × 24.

81. *Yard Talk*. Martha's Vineyard, Massachusetts.
Watercolor. 1978. 20 × 32.
Collection of Mr. and Mrs. G. D. Conover.

82. *Picnic at Chappaquiddick*. Martha's Vineyard, Massachusetts. Watercolor. 1984. 6½ × 10.

83. *The Naushon*. Woods Hole, Massachusetts. Watercolor. 1985. 6½ × 14.

84. *White Dory*. Penobscot Bay, Maine. Watercolor. 1985. 24 × 38.

85. *Winter Comes*. Eastport, Maine. Watercolor. 1985. 11 × 11.

86. *Behind the Shed*. Monhegan Island, Maine. Watercolor. 1984. 10 × 17.

87. *Boiling Surf*. Maine. Watercolor. 1977. 17 × 28.

88. *Christmas Cove*. Christmas Cove, Maine. Watercolor. 1985. 17½ × 25.

89. *Morning Caller*. Friendship, Maine. Watercolor. 1979. 15½ × 28. Private Collection.

90. *Near Thomaston*. Thomaston, Maine. Watercolor. 1972. 13½ × 21. Collection of Mr. and Mrs. Lloyd Field.

91. *Puffins*. Maine. Watercolor. 1985. 8 × 12.

92. *Loon*. Maine. Watercolor. 1985. 9 × 13½.

93. *Homage to Homer*. Prouts Neck, Maine. Oil. 1984. 20 × 24.

94. *Gibby Alley . . . Lobsterman*. Jonesport, Maine. Watercolor. 1984. 12 × 8.

95. *Rolling In*. Penobscot Bay, Maine. Watercolor. 1972. 21½ × 24½. Collection of Ben Swanson.

96. *Poppies*. Penobscot Bay, Maine. Watercolor. 1972. 16 × 17¼. Private Collection.

97. *The Sailmaker*. Blue Hill, Maine. Watercolor. 1985. 24 × 36. Collection of Mr. and Mrs. Gene Simpson.

98. *Lash's Boatyard*. Friendship, Maine. Watercolor. 1971. 6½ × 19. Collection of Ben Swanson.

99. *Lobsterman's Cove*. Penobscot Bay, Maine. Watercolor. 1980. 21½ × 36. Collection of Johnson & Higgins.

100. *The Privy*. Penobscot Bay, Maine. Watercolor. 1972. 10¾ × 9. Private Collection.

101. *Raspberries*. Maine. Watercolor. 1982. 13¼ × 22½.

102. *Seal Cove*. Penobscot Bay, Maine. Watercolor. 1977. 12 × 20. Private Collection.

103. *Foul-Weather Gear*. Penobscot Bay, Maine. Watercolor. 1978. 13 × 20½. Private Collection.

104. *Meadow by the Church*. Jonesport, Maine. Watercolor. 1984. 23 × 37. Private Collection.

105. *Winter's Wood*. Eastport, Maine. Watercolor. 1984. 24 × 38¼.

106. *Rebuilding at Jonesport*. Jonesport, Maine. Oil. 1985. 40 × 48.

107. *Island Overlook*. Penobscot Bay, Maine. Watercolor. 1973. 17 × 33. Collection of Allied-Signal Inc.

108. *Root Cellar*. Winter Harbor, Maine. Watercolor. 1984. 19½ × 25¼.

109. *Breaking Through*. Monhegan Island, Maine. Oil. 1985. 30 × 40. Collection of the Artist.

110. *Manana Island Sketch*. Manana Island, Maine. Watercolor. 1984. 7 × 14. Private Collection.

Designed by
Bob Nance

Text composed in Linotron Bembo by
Akra Data
Birmingham, Alabama

Color separations by
Pinaire Lithographing Corporation
Louisville, Kentucky

Printed and bound by
Arcata Graphics—Kingsport
Kingsport, Tennessee

Text sheets are Sterling Litho Matte by
Westvāco
New York, New York

Endleaves are
Carnival® Cover by
Champion International Corporation
Stamford, Connecticut

Cover cloth is Payko by
The Holliston Mills, Inc.
Kingsport, Tennessee

110. *Manana Island Sketch.*

Bangor
Machias
Eastport
Ellsworth
Jonesport
Belfast
Castine
Camden
Mt. Desert
Blue Hill Bay
Rockland
Penobscot Bay
Bath
Matinicus
Monhegan
Portland
Casco Bay
Cape Elizabeth
Muscongus Bay
Portsmouth
Isles of Shoals
Cape Ann
Gloucester
Boston
Plymouth
Provincetown
Cape Cod Bay
Providence
Chatham
New London
Newport
New Haven
Cuttyhunk
Martha's Vineyard
Nantucket
New York
Long Island Sound
Block Is.
Montauk
Great So. Bay
Sandy Hook
Philadelphia
Barnegat Inlet
Atlantic City